HUGS, HOPE, AND AND PEANUT BUTTER

FINDING THE LIGHT BEHIND THE CLOUDS

HUGS, HOPE, AND PEANUT BUTTER

ILLUSTRATED BY CRITICALLY ILL CHILDREN

MARSHA JORDAN

CREATOR OF THE HUGS AND HOPE FOUNDATION

JADA

This book is a work of nonfiction.

Published in 2006 by JADA Press
Jacksonville, Florida
www.JadaPress.com

ISBN: 0-9771343-4-2

Cover Art & Design:
Jamon Walker, Mythic Design Studio
www.mythicstudio.com

Interior Design & Formatting:
Carolyn White, BookMakers Ink
www.bookmakersink.com

Printed in the United States of America

ACKNOWLEDGMENTS

Except where otherwise noted, Scripture passages are taken from the New International Version of the Bible copyright 1973, 1978, 1984 by International Bible Society.

New American Standard Bible copyright 1960, 1962, 1963, 1968, 1971, 1972, 1973, 1975, 1977 by The Lockman Foundation.

Today's English Version (The Good News Bible) copyright 1966, 1971, 1992. American Bible Society.

The New Testament In Modern English by J.B. Phillips Copyright © J.B. Phillips 1958, 1959, 1960, 1972 Macmillan Publishing Company

Contemporary English Version Copyright © 1995 by American Bible Society. Used by permission

DEDICATIONS

This book is dedicated to the memory of Nance Olive who lost her battle to cancer on May 5, 2004, at the young age of forty-seven. This awesome lady was a courageous and joyful Christian who inspired all those with whom she came into contact. I was blessed to know her, and I look forward to seeing her beautiful smile again some day when we meet in heaven.

Nance believed the most important thing she'd learned in life was how essential forgiveness is, not only to give but to receive. She told me about how God had enabled her to forgive others and herself for past hurts and mistakes. That forgiveness gave her peace and led to relationships that were a great blessing to her. But what gave her the greatest happiness was knowing that God had forgiven her. Just before she died, Nance told me, "I still cry when I think about God forgiving me. Something people don't realize and that people need to remember is that God is with us all the time and everywhere, bringing us to places and people that we need in our lives." Nance never doubted God's presence and His working in her life. That was obvious by the peace she felt in her heart and the faith she demonstrated by her actions.

"Your son has cancer." Those words are devastating for any parent. It was no different for Mary and Chuck Bryce of New York. First their nine-year-old son, Justin, had a liver transplant. Then the cancer went into his lungs and he had lung surgery. When the cancer spread to Justin's brain, his family was devastated and once again Justin needed surgery. Tumors continued to grow in spite of the surgery, chemotherapy, and radiation. After a valiant fight, this brave little soldier passed away at the age of ten, on Christmas Day, 2003, in his mother's arms.

REVIEWS

"Marsha Jordan writes with purpose and conviction and an unfailing sense of humor. You'll soon be laughing out loud and won't want to put this book down! Be prepared to come away with a great sense of hope and quite possibly the same sense of joy and conviction that Jordan shares with every story. A very timely book from a very gifted Christian writer."

Lisa Barker (www.JellyMom.com)

"With wit and biblical wisdom that few have mastered well, Marsha Jordan expresses the reality of day-to-day struggles and joys with laugh-out-loud humor while reminding us that God walks beside us through life's most difficult circumstances. Her amazing attitude and exceptional experiences prove that prayer and a laugh a day keep hope from fading away. A must read!"
Donna Wyland, Founder and Director of Foundation of Hope

"Marsha Jordan has written a fabulous compilation of essays that will touch your soul with both laughter and tears. By sharing her personal experiences, weaknesses, and hard-learned wisdom with charming candor, Jordan will teach you how to incorporate God's message of hope and healing in your own life. Her hilarious stories about her dog Louie and her "very male" husband will keep you amused all the way to the end. This book is a must-read for women who love to laugh and who believe in the power of hugs and hope."
Vicky DeCoster
Author of *The Wacky World of Womanhood: Essays on Girlhood, Dating, Motherhood, and the Loss of Underwear.*
(www.wackywomanhood.com)

"Author Marsha Jordan uplifts your faith and lightens your day with her humorous stories about family life. Moreover, the founder of the Hugs and Hope nonprofit organization, which helps sick children and their families, has included angel stories of how people help each other. Marsha reminds us that acts of kindness aren't random, but fostered through good hearts and real action. She provides wit instead of worry and reminds us that we are fine just the way we are. She exemplifies being real and down-to-earth in the stories, and refreshingly gives readers permission to be themselves. An enjoyable read!"

Dr. Caron Goode, Founder
Academy for Coaching Parents International, LLC
(www.acpi.biz)

PREFACE

Have you ever been depressed or discouraged? Do you get tired of struggling with the difficulties of life? Are you ever so disappointed and frustrated that you want to give up?

Like you, I understand disappointment, frustration, and depression. As a result of illness and disability, I have experienced many losses—loss of a job, loss of ability, loss of hobbies, energy, income, and even friends. At times I have even lost my self-esteem and hope itself. I've asked the same questions you ask: Is there a purpose in suffering? Who is to blame? What do I do with my questions? How do I find strength to cope?

For years, pain and exhaustion have been my constant companions. However, I also have another companion who never leaves me, and that is God. He meets me at the difficult points in life. He stays with me through troubles. He not only offers comfort and strength, but He teaches me in the process. My doubts lead me to seek Him more than I would otherwise. As a result, He's better able to teach me about His character and His purposes.

Through challenges to my faith, I've discovered that God's plan for my life is often very different from my own. My intent with this book is to share my experiences, my faith, and the lessons I've learned from the wisdom of the Bible.

I haven't answered the tough questions. I haven't revealed any great new insights, but as you read about my journey, perhaps you will discover the healing power of humor and faith. I offer you hope and the opportunity to face difficulties with a smile.

I hope you will find encouragement and perseverance—even in the midst of sorrow and pain. I hope you will be comforted as I share what I believe so that you may draw upon it when you face tough times. I hope you will learn to laugh, as I make fun of myself and my circumstances; and I hope to share with you God's message that you need never face hardships alone.

I will have succeeded in my mission if this book helps you see struggles from a new perspective, renews your trust in God, and encourages you to move forward with a smile.

INTRODUCTION

I thought you should know a little about me before reading my book. The easiest way to introduce myself is to say simply that I'm the three F's. Fat, female, and fifty.

I like puppies, funny movies, and birthday extravaganzas at Chuck E. Cheese. Hallmark's crabby old lady, Maxine, is my mentor. I hate spiders, cigarettes, and empty toilet paper rolls. I eat just about anything that doesn't run from me, and I have varicose veins, which, if stretched end to end, would reach to Madagascar.

My favorite sport is surfing the web. Other hobbies include snoring, nagging the husband, riding my pet pig Luke Skywalker, and ignoring my dirty windows.

TURNING FIFTY

As I said before, I'm fifty. That's three-hundred and fifty in dog years. While fifty may be young for a tortoise or a tree, it feels very old to me, and it ranks right up there with slamming my lips in the car door, squirting vomit out my nose, and selling my kidneys to pay off credit card debt.

Turning fifty hasn't stifled my immaturity, but it's been traumatic nevertheless. On the fiftieth anniversary of my natal day, I cried nonstop and consumed twenty seven Hershey bars to console myself. I just hope I'll be able to lead a meaningful life into my early sixties.

I realize there are many famous people who accomplished great things in their old age. John Glenn for instance. He was seventy-seven when he took his last trip into space. At that age, anybody would rather be flying above the earth than lying under it. Then there's Whistler's mother. Oh, wait a minute. She didn't do anything but sit in the rocking chair while her son painted her. Well, what about George Burns? He lived to a ripe old age and remained funny up to the end. I can do that. People say I'm pretty funny when I simultaneously sneeze and wet my pants.

To celebrate being half a century old, I had a hysterectomy. When the doctor cut me open, he found a few teeth, three marbles, and eighty-seven cents that I had swallowed as a child. The operation was a success, but the doctor told me not to climb stairs. That's frustrating because climbing up that drain pipe is no picnic. The doctor did say I'd be normal soon. I'm looking forward to that, since I've never been normal before.

Over the years, I've enjoyed many unusual jobs, like head inspector at the flea dip factory, dance hall girl, and Phyllis Diller's stunt double; but I prefer the stimulation and excitement of being an unknown writer. I'm realistic enough to know I'll never be a famous author, but that's only because I have to maintain a low profile. I'm a fugitive due to some library books that I (allegedly) never returned, back in high school.

In my fifty years, I've done a lot. Besides being a Sunday school teacher, a Boy Scout leader, a reading tutor, a home-schooling mom, and a publicist, I've been a 4-H leader, a real estate analyst, an administrative assistant, a hospital registrar, an Avon lady, a Hallmark store clerk, check out lady in a grocery store, a Shaklee distributor, a Home Interiors Demonstrator, a supper club hostess, and a preschool teacher. Whew!

Because of my age (old) and my vast experience, I feel not only entitled but compelled to give advice to friends, family, and strangers on the street. I am, after all, the most astute and sagacious dame in the world. As leader of the local Know-it-alls Anonymous Club, I believe I know EVERYTHING. Oh no, I've become my mother!

A few years ago, I was in a serious accident, and they tell me one lobe of my brain doesn't work right anymore. That explains why I put the phone in the fridge, try to call friends using the remote control, and can't remember anything dating back farther than two p.m. yesterday. Since my accident, getting behind the wheel is scary, especially in snowy weather. I am doing better, though. I can drive up to forty miles per hour now, and next I'll work on opening my eyes.

BEING FAT

People try to avoid the subject, but I am not shy about discussing my fat. I am twice the woman I used to be, but I figure even my blubber serves a purpose. Other people feel better when they stand next to me. I imagine them saying, "Well, at least I am skinnier than that."

Except for the fact that I cannot carry a tune, I would have made a great opera singer. I have the body; all I need now is one of those hats with the horns.

I received an email today with a subject line that read "Erase Ugly Cellulite Today." I deleted it. Even if the advertising were true, I wouldn't use the stuff. If I lost all my body fat, there would be nothing left of me!

Being fat is a handy excuse for not doing things you really don't want to do anyway. For instance, I no longer wear pantyhose. I kept tripping over the crotch, and the last time I wrestled a pair on, the workout was so hard, I ended up in the emergency room.

Sure, being fat has its disadvantages, such as my stomach reaching the shower several minutes before the rest of my body does, but there are advantages too. My stomach keeps my knees warm and shields them from spilled spaghetti sauce, and it comes in handy as a serving tray.

I've been on a diet since the seventh grade and I've lost the same 30 pounds approximately sixty-seven times. If I hadn't gained them all back, I'd be small enough now to travel in the glove compartment of my car and take a bath in the cup holder.

The husband and I both try to avoid fatty things; but it's difficult since we live in a small apartment and keep running into each other. Maybe we could win this battle of the bulge if someone would just invent fat-free butter, meat free Big Macs, chocolate free chocolates, and lettuce that tastes like pizza. Meanwhile, I'm considering treating myself to massive plastic surgery. I wonder if there is such a thing as full-body lyposuction.

For years, I've suffered with a connective tissue disease, migraines, fibromyalgia, and chronic fatigue. Some part of my body always hurts, and dialing long distance wears me out. I get short of breath from chewing gum, so you can imagine how I feel about exercising. The most activity I get is aerobic eating and breathing in place. Nevertheless, I should be able to touch my toes again soon, I just have to grow my fingernails another ten inches.

MY LIFE

I've battled depression most of my adult life. In fact, several times I came close to winning an award for the longest depression in history. This year I came in second only because the first place winner was a ninety-year-old grandmother whose post-partum blues spanned six decades. I have won my share of other awards, though, such as the county hog calling and seed-spitting contests and burping competitions at the fair.

I've been held hostage for more than twenty years in the north woods of Wisconsin—the booming metropolis of Harshaw, to be exact. That's where the weasels and wood ticks roam and where winter never ends. As a domestic diva, I lead an exciting life with all the glamor of an enema.

I'm married to a man who's been stuck in a mid-life crisis since the Nixon administration. His nickname is H.M., which stands for Hunky Magoo. He likes to think it stands for His Majesty. I have other pet names I like to call him, but this is a "G" rated book, so I can't print them here. I tell people that I used to live life in the fast lane till I married a speed bump.

I can't believe we've stayed together thirty years even though we're incompatible. It's amazing what intensive therapy, sheer will power, and modern drugs can accomplish. I have to say, though, that as we get older we do get along better. We're both too old and tired to throw knick knacks, furniture, or appliances at each other anymore.

Ours is what's been called a give and take relationship. He gives orders and I take out Chinese for supper.

One threat to our marriage has been my snoring. The husband claims it blows his toupee off his head and sounds as if I'm sleeping with three kazoos up my nose. If snoring were a competitive sport, I could win trophies. But when it comes to relationships, sounding like a rooting pig doesn't exactly encourage romance. It tends to drive a wedge between spouses. However, I daily remind the husband that, when we were married, he vowed to love me from that day snoreward.

On our thirtieth anniversary, we couldn't afford much of a celebration, although the husband frequently reminds me that we have all the money we'll ever need. Yeah, sure, if we become street people and live in a Frigidaire box.

To celebrate our anniversary, Captain Spendo took me to his favorite restaurant and told me to order the most expensive item on the menu. So I had a Big Mac.

Then we took a romantic vacation to a Prozac mine in Sheboygan. The drive there was a little stressful. I had to wear ear plugs, because riding with the husband is like being confined with an auctioneer who has Tourette Syndrome. Once we got to our destination, though, we had a blast sampling newly developed products like Prozac pancake syrup, Prozac toothpaste, and Prozac hair spray. My favorite is the pez-shaped Prozac candy. It comes with a cute dispenser. On top is a screaming person pulling out his hair. After spitting out the candy, the head spins and shoots off into space. What'll they think of next?

MY FAMILY

The husband and I were married in 1975. Before our first child was born in 1976, we had decided to name him Horace—even if he was a girl. After seeing him, though, we didn't think he looked like a Horace. We considered other names like Bowlegged Benny or Twelve Toed Timmy, but we ended up calling him Hunky Magoo Junior.

I've known this kid for a very long time. Yet I was unaware that he was a talented musician until after he made his first CD. Who woulda thought? Now we're just waiting for him to become filthy rich so we can move in and sponge off him.

When our son was twenty years old, we adopted another child—a cute little eight-pound, curly haired, black boy. His name is Louie and he's a toy poodle with the I.Q. of liver. He's about as well-liked too. He recently had most of his teeth pulled, so now we call him the toothless wonder dog. He's the world's lickingest and stupidest dog. Lucky for him he's cute. It's his one and only redeeming quality.

The light of my life is our delightful grandson, Cobi. He is God's reward for surviving my son. Stories about Cobi are sprinkled throughout this book. I don't understand why he hasn't been named a national treasure yet, but he's precious to us. I love being a grandma and carrying pictures where my money used to be. I can whip out my eighty-seven page brag book faster than Wyatt Erp drew his gun. I wonder if that's why friends cross over to the opposite side of the street when they see me coming.

MY STORIES

A major life adjustment for me came in 1998 when a flare up of my illness caused temporary blindness. After a simple surgery, what was supposed to be a three-day recovery turned into a three-month nightmare. During that time, I had a daily to-do list of only three things: get up, survive, and go to bed. I'm still suffering the effects of that ordeal, but that's a story for later in this book.

My stories, by the way, are true. I'm not clever enough to create fiction that's as funny as my life. I may have exaggerated just a tad here and there to make things slightly more interesting, so I guess you can say the stories are mostly true but partly fiction. After all, who would pay money to read boring stuff? And I do need the money so I can send large donations annually to the Foundation for Cognitively Challenged and Abandoned Toy Poodles with Personality Disorders and Bladder Control Problems. That's where I got my dog.

I suggest that you take what's written in this book with a grain of salt and maybe some Ex-lax. A couple of Alka Seltzer couldn't hurt either, if reading this makes you sick.

I enjoyed writing this book because it took me away from the drudgery of cooking and cleaning, which I've successfully avoided for more than three years. It's my first book, but several of my other writings already appear on restroom walls across the country. If you actually like what you read here, you're among a small group of eccentric people, so drop me a note and let me know you exist. I need mail, since I burn it to heat my office.

Now that you know a little about me, you should be adequately prepared to read my essays. Hang on to your knickers. Here we go.

Life iz a conztant battle between celery and chocolate.

TABLE OF CONTENTS

CHAPTER ONE

CHAPTER TWO

CHAPTER THREE

CHAPTER FOUR

CHAPTER FIVE

The Gain of Loss

(Making a turn around)

CHAPTER SIX

Triumph in Trials

(Turning Stumbling Blocks Into Stepping Stones)

CHAPTER SEVEN

CHAPTER EIGHT

CHAPTER ONE

I'M NOT OKAY, YOU'RE NOT OKAY, BUT THAT'S OKAY

Nothing in the world can separate you from the love of God.

(Romans 8:39)

IF HE ONLY HAD A BRAIN

When people ask me if my dog is a mutt, I tell them, "No, he's a moron."

King Louie is a nine-year-old, twelve-pound toy poodle who has the intelligence of rock salt. The day we brought him home, the husband and I decided to name him Zippy; but within hours, we realized that name did not suit him.

On his first day of obedience class, the instructor informed me that Louie was untrainable. That was just after she ripped out most of her hair and right before she called him a Jell-O brain and ran from the building sobbing. Louie not only flunked the class, he was dishonorably discharged.

We dubbed the cantankerous canine King Louie, not because of his regal demeanor or his majestic appearance. He earned that title because of his overbearing ways. The domineering little devil rules our home with an iron paw. He demands absolute respect from his human subjects. Louie changes from cute little fur ball into ferocious beast in 3.5 milliseconds when someone attempts to usurp his authority. He snarls viciously at those who dare to extricate him from his couch throne.

Besides being a control freak with a brain the size of a Rice Krispy, King Louie is a loner. He hates drop in guests—or any guests for that matter. Perhaps his disagreeable temper is the result of painful periodontal disease. Either that, or he's not getting enough fiber in his diet. For whatever reason, the toothless little tyrant discourages intruders by baring his shriveled gums and growling obscenities.

Though his domain covers forty wooded acres, the King doesn't roam very far from home. In fact, he doesn't care to go outside much at all, especially unescorted. And he is adamant about not venturing forth in the rain. It takes three sumo wrestlers to force this dwarf of a dog out the door during inclement weather. Being a passive aggressive pooch, Louie retaliates by relieving himself on the front porch.

Louie has made his mark—several in fact—not on the world, but in our home. Though he can roam free in our three-thousand square foot, two-story house, when he feels the urge to throw up or have an uncontrollable bout of explosive diarrhea, he heads straight for the oriental rug. If we toss him outside, he stands staring at the door until we let him back in. Once inside, he picks up where he left off and resumes spurting something out from one end or the other. Louie faithfully obeys the doggie code of ethics which lists rule number one as never regurgitate outside. The mangy monarch monopolizes my bed and whines at the bathroom door when I'm in the tub. He jumps on my lap when I'm typing, and he watches me when I go to the bathroom. He clings to me like a hair on a grilled cheese sandwich.

Louie's favorite bone is my ankle. After nine years of intensive training, he hasn't yet learned to sit. In fact, he barely knows how to stand. However, he does respond to a few voice commands. For instance, when I say "come," he instantly runs in the opposite direction. When I say "stay," he leaps up and attaches himself leech-like to my thigh. When I order him to "heel," he gnaws on my shoes. When he chases cars and I yell, "No!" he immediately steps up his pace. I can't get him to fetch either. The only stick he's interested in is a bread stick, and the only balls he'll chase are meatballs.

I think the problem is that Louie doesn't understand English. Since poodles come from France, I tried speaking French to him.

Who knew he wasn't bi-lingual? I said "oui oui" and he did just that! So now I'm taking French lessons so I can communicate with him in his native tongue.

This high-strung hound turns up his royal nose at milk bone biscuits and dog chow, preferring instead french fries, cherries jubilee, and linguine in clam sauce. This is one thing we have in common. In fact, we're a lot alike in the eating department.

Neither of us relishes what is nutritious, and we both occasionally eat till we're sick. I, however, do not gobble food whole or throw up twice my body weight—in bed. Neither do I stubbornly plant myself under the dining room table while whining, yipping, and drooling throughout the meal. I also refuse to ingest paper plates, no matter how sumptuous they smell; and I would never curl up on dirty underwear and nibble on my husband's feet.

Recently, His Peskiness accompanied us on a long car trip. A very long trip. At least it seemed to last forever. This was supposed to be a relaxing vacation? Louie refused to sit anywhere in the car but on my lap. During the six hour trip, he busied himself by jumping in my face, licking my face, and breathing in my face. He also whined non-stop except during an occasional break or two to lick the windows.

Riding in the car is one of Louie's favorite pastimes. Or at least he bounds enthusiastically into the car in anticipation of the ride. He believes very strongly that he must accompany us everywhere. After all, you never know when you might need a tiny demon dog to pant and bark violently at nothing right in your ear while he's walking on your chest as you speed down the expressway.

The only thing Louie likes better than getting into the car is getting out. Once we leave the driveway, the pitiful whining begins and doesn't stop till the car door opens, allowing his escape.

You can always tell when Louie's been in the car. The windows are coated with dog slobber and the vehicle smells like a combination of moldy swamp water, an old bowling shoe, and a backed up toilet.

Besides road trips, other things Louie enjoys are marking his territory when new furniture is added to our home; sitting in the middle of a room full of company and licking himself; barking incessantly at invisible monsters; violently charging the poor UPS man; emitting fowl odors; and ignoring everything spoken by his master, with the exception of the words "treat," and "yummies."

A pomegranate is smarter than Crazy Louie (a.k.a. Nutsie) and any self respecting fruit would be insulted to be compared with him. The runt is fortunate that he's cute. If not for his floppy ears and that helpless, innocent look, he would never have survived this long.

The only reason we have endured the Doofus for nine years is because we're certain no normal family would tolerate his obnoxious behavior. We feel sorry for him because he is brain damaged and ill mannered. We believe that his inner puppy may have been traumatized early in life, warping his personality and making his applesauce brain psychopathic. We spoil him rotten, because we feel sorry for him. He's treated better than most children, and nothing is expected of him. He doesn't even take out the garbage.

I've tried several times to give Louie away, but at the last minute, I always back out due to guilt. I just know that any other owner would surely abuse him because he would drive them mad. When we're tempted to get rid of him, we always reconsider after thinking about what a new owner might do when the little creep not only bites the hand that feeds him, but takes a leak on his clean laundry, eats his underwear, and barfs on his pillow.

So, we've kept Louie all these years, not because we love him—just to protect him from an early entrance to doggie heaven. Although, if such a place does exist, I seriously doubt that Louie would be allowed in.

Speaking of heaven, how fortunate we humans are that we don't have to rely upon our good behavior or lovability to get into "people heaven." God's greatest desire is that we will spend eternity there with Him. Like Louie, we too can often be obnoxious and unlovable. Yet, Jesus was willing to die for us! You can believe that God cares deeply about you. The apostle John wrote: *"How great is the love the Father has lavished on us."* (1 John 3:1)

No one is unlovable to God, and no one can out sin His mercy

King Louie by Christi T.

WHAT ARE YOU WORTH?

My husband and I collect antiques and often argue about their value. He'll say, "This is worth five-hundred dollars." And my reply is "It's not worth anything unless someone is willing to buy it."

People put great value on things. I laugh at how much some folks pay for little trinkets such as old eggbeaters or broken toys like those I played with as a child. (Yes, my old toys are collectable antiques now. Isn't that a cheery thought?) A lot of the stuff in antique shops looks like junk I'd throw away. I wouldn't take those things if they were free—and I certainly wouldn't pay for them. But they are valuable to dealers and collectors, the people who are willing to pay big bucks for anything old. Beauty and worth, after all, are in the eye of the beholder.

I heard about a man who computed his taxes and discovered that he owed over three-thousand dollars. He sent a letter to the IRS that said, "Enclosed is my tax return and payment. Please take note of the attached article from USA Today. In the article, you will see that the Pentagon is paying one-hundred and seventy-one dollars for hammers and NASA paid six-hundred dollars for a toilet seat. Please find enclosed four toilet seats and six hammers." Wouldn't you love to pay taxes that way? Obviously, toilet seats and hammers, no matter how nice they are, are not worth this much to anybody except the government.

Nothing is worth more than what someone's willing to pay for it. Even your worth is determined by how much someone would pay. And someone did willingly pay an outlandish price for you. *"The Son of Man did not come to be served, but to serve, and to give His life as a ransom for many."* (Mark 10:45)

God values you so much that He paid the price of his own son's life for you. You are, as the credit card commercial says, "priceless."

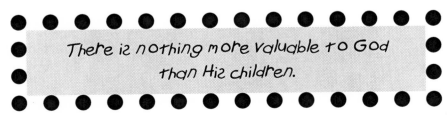

There is nothing more valuable to God than His children.

PURSE HUNT

Way back B.C. (before children), I had a purse to match every outfit, including the pink suede purse that went with my pink patent leather heels. Yeah, you heard that right. I was a real fashion diva.

Now that I'm older, wiser, frazzled, frenzied, and exhausted, I don't have time to coordinate my wardrobe. I've become a one-purse woman. That one purse serves as my carryall for everything I might need. I use it till the straps fall off; so it's essential to find just the right, perfect purse—and that is no easy task.

Being a modern grandma on the go, I practically live in my car, so I must be prepared for any emergency. Therefore, in my purse, I carry a supply of each of my eighty-nine medications, along with cosmetics for touch ups, toiletries and snacks in case I'm stranded overnight, and books to read while waiting in line. It holds a night gown for emergency overnighters as well as my digital camera and my video camera, in case I have a Kodak moment.

I stock my purse with plenty of quarters for video games and soda machines (for my grandson) an extra pair of pantyhose (for me, not him) and several changes of underwear (for both of us). I stuff in silverware, straws and napkins (those fast food places often forget these). I include a rain hat, umbrella, and plastic poncho for inclement weather.

Also in my purse are sun screen and hand cream, cough drops, eye drops, ear drops and gum drops, bug spray, nasal spray, hair spray, and pepper spray, scotch tape and duct tape, a first aid kit, a sewing kit, a tool kit, and a pool repair kit. Oh, and an inflatable raft. You never know when you might fall overboard.

I recently spent an entire day scrutinizing each item in Wal-Mart's purse department. After an exhausting search, I finally ferreted out the perfect purse. It had twenty-nine compartments and was large enough to hold all my necessities, plus a liter of Dr. Pepper and a portable television set. I couldn't wait to transfer my treasures from the old, ratty, strapless bag to my dream purse.

Embarking upon a shopping marathon the next morning, I was grief-stricken when I realized I didn't have the muscles to lug the huge thing around. Since acquiring my new purse, I've developed low back pain, a perpetual stiff neck, and tennis elbow from hoisting the sucker over my shoulder. And I think I need a rotator cuff transplant. The only things this almost-ideal purse lacks are wheels to drag it along behind me.

Against my better judgement, I took my new purse with me on a cross-country trip. How dare the airline personnel accuse me of smuggling in carry-on baggage that was larger than the overhead compartment! When I refused to give up my doghouse sized purse, they reluctantly allowed me onboard with the stipulation that I must hold it on my lap. Because the monstrosity weighs more than I do, my legs were numb during the entire flight.

What a let down. I thought that I'd at last found the ideal purse—only to discover that it's not so perfect after all. If Wal-Mart won't take it back, it will go into the trash compactor.

I'm certainly glad that God doesn't act toward me the way I act with my purses! I search for perfection, but He accepts imperfection. I'm looking for something to fill my needs. He looks for someone who has needs He can fill. When I disappoint God, He doesn't toss me back and look for something better. He said, *"I've chosen you. I'll never throw you away."* (Isaiah 41:9)

God cherishes all of us imperfect people. Or should I say purse-ons? No matter what size, shape, or color, He loves and accepts us. He doesn't care how much we can carry or how organized we are. It doesn't matter if we can't fill every need ourselves. He loves us each for who we are—His children. And He makes up for what we lack. *"The Lord is good and His love endures forever."* (Psalm 100)

Jeremiah 31:3 says: *"I have loved you with an everlasting love."* I'm reminded of God's awesome love every time I swing my gigantic purse over my sore shoulder.

Purse by Rachel S.

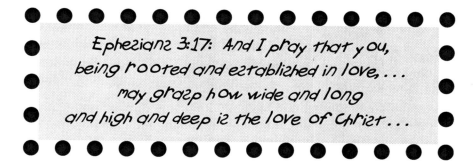

Ephesians 3:17: And I pray that you, being rooted and established in love, . . . may grasp how wide and long and high and deep is the love of Christ . . .

THINGS THAT GO BARF IN THE NIGHT

I have difficulty sleeping because my dog shares my bed. When I say "shares," I mean he assigns me a tiny space on the edge where I must hang on with my toenails to keep from falling out. Louie stretches out sideways in the middle of the bed and hogs the pillow, growling in his sleep if I try to claim a corner of it for myself.

The worst part about sleeping with Louie is the racket his stomach makes. Like the ghost of Jacob Marley, it haunts my dreams. The gurgles, growls, and roars are loud enough to break the smell barrier. Sometimes I wake up to so much noise I think I'm in the middle of Mardi Gras.

The other night, when I finally managed to go to sleep, I had a dream that started out great. I was happily driving my hot pink Cadillac convertible to a rubber stampers' convention. Out of nowhere came another car and bam! I ran right into it. A policeman arrived on the scene within seconds—because he was driving the car I hit. Boy, was I glad to wake up from that dream!

Many of my dreams end badly. That's because Louie not only torments me during waking hours; but he crashes my dreams and ruins those too. I hate it when he has seizures, asthma attacks, and digestive disturbances in the middle of the night. It's hard to sleep with someone jerking, hacking, and wheezing in your ear. Especially when that someone's breath smells like an anchovy cannery. Somehow, what's going on in my conscious world gets mixed up with my unconscious thoughts and incorporated into my dream.

It's really annoying when this happens during the best part of a Mel Gibson dream! The scenario goes something like this:

Mel: "I beg of you. You must be my leading lady. * Cough.* No one else can take your place."

Me: "Oh, Mel. You're making me blush!"

Mel: * Wheeze* "I must have you. * Snort* If you refuse, I'll go on a hunger strike—. Haaaack!"

Me: "What was that Mel? I didn't catch that last part."

Mel: "Hornnnk! Gag. Honnnkkk!"

Me: "Mel, you smell like a pig farmer's boots—hey! Don't lick my face, Mel. Wait, what are you doing? Not on my pillow!"

Mel: " Blaaaaagh! Caahaaack!"

Then I usually awake in time to catch Louie hacking up cricket legs, bits of candy wrapper, or the half-digested remains of a paper plate.

I hate having my sleep disrupted, because the only hope I have of meeting Mel Gibson is in my dreams. I do a lot of other impossible things in my dreams too, like flying without an airplane, and walking around in the mall wearing nothing but my underwear.

I have other dreams that, though seemingly impossible, are attainable, and not just when I'm asleep. For instance, I have the hope of not only rising from the dead someday, but of living forever and having an incorruptible, healthy (and hopefully thin) body. I dream of being united with loved ones in heaven and living there forever in the presence of God. Meeting Him will be even better than co-starring with Mel Gibson!

Louie by Caleb L

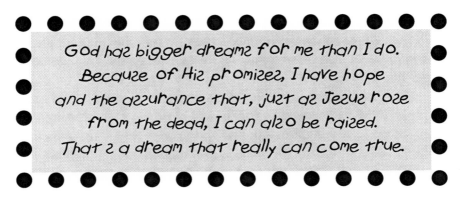

God has bigger dreams for me than I do.
Because of His promises, I have hope
and the assurance that, just as Jesus rose
from the dead, I can also be raised.
That's a dream that really can come true.

GIMME, GIMME, GIMME

Sometimes I feel sorry for my dog. He stands less than a foot tall, and resembles a guinea pig with an afro. He spends most of his waking hours scurrying around at my feet and straining his neck, looking up to see what I'm doing. He's always hoping I'll drop some tasty morsel; and when I do, he's ready to snatch it.

When I complain about Louie being under foot, the husband reminds me how tough it must be for such a little guy living in a giants' world. I guess in Louie's eyes, I must look like a mountain.

There is a whole big world that I can see, which is unknown to Louie. He sees mostly ankles and toes. It's the same way with me and God. I see only what's right around me; but God sees a larger picture. With my limited view of things, I often see no way out of problems. Just like my little dog, I need someone bigger to help me find my way. Problems that look like insurmountable mountains to me are like tiny ant hills to God.

I often tell Louie how lucky he is to have me as his master, because I spoil him and take good care of him. Of course, he doesn't understand. He wags his tail, tilts his head, and gives me what I call the "gimme gimme look." It's that goofy expression of expectation that says, "What do you have for me? I want it. Can I have it? Gimme, gimme, gimme. Give it to me *Now!*"

One day, as I looked down at Louie, I realized that I am much more like him than I'd like to admit (except that I don't roll in dead, smelly things). I too cannot even begin to understand the goodness of my master or fully appreciate all that He does for me.

Like Louie, I spend a lot of time whining for more and expecting a never ending supply of treats to satisfy my selfish desires—instead of thanking God for what He's already given me.

I'm glad I'm not a dog—for many reasons, not the least of which is that I can take a shower instead of—well, you know what dogs do!

But I'm especially thankful that, though I am a small speck in the universe, I have a BIG God who doesn't expect more from me than I can give.

And when problems become too huge for me to handle, I remember that God promised He would always be there for me, as well as for everybody who loves and seeks Him.

Isaiah 43:1-4 says, *"But now, this is what the LORD says . . . 'Fear not . . . When you walk through the fire, you will not be burned; the flames will not set you ablaze. For I am the LORD, your God, the Holy One of Israel, your Savior'"*

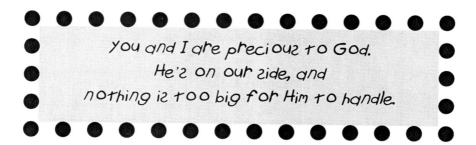

You and I are precious to God.
He's on our side, and
nothing is too big for Him to handle.

Louie by Steven S.

NOW I SEE

Due to complications of a connective tissue disease, without warning I'd been struck blind. Doctors tried treatment after treatment, in a race to stop the damage to my eyes before it was too late. After each daily examination, the cornea specialist would hold his hand in front of my face and ask how many fingers I could see. Hope dwindled, as day after day I replied, "none."

As I lay awake in the lonely darkness, I prayed harder than I'd ever prayed before. The last several weeks, I had been living in the middle of my most dreaded nightmare. I felt alone, frustrated, sad, and afraid. All my plans and dreams for the future were hanging by a thin thread that could break at any moment.

The searing pain stabbed at my eyes. It felt as if fire were consuming them. But it wasn't pain that caused my sleeplessness. Worse than the excruciating physical torment was the terrifying darkness and the agonizing over the "what if's."

What if I accidentally pulled the protective coverings off in my sleep and rubbed my eyes against the pillow? The doctor had warned me to avoid even a slight touch to my inflamed corneas.

What if I would never regain my sight? What if I couldn't take care of myself? What if I couldn't drive my car and be independent anymore? What if I would never enjoy reading a book, watching a sunset, or—worst of all—gazing into the eyes of my beautiful grandbaby?

During the long, sleepless nights, I fumed in disbelief, "Why is this happening? I can't be permanently blinded!" In despair, I cried silently in my heart, questioning God. But I had to hold back the tears because crying irritated my eyes more.

Besides the torturous pain and the devastating fear of not regaining my vision, there was the anxiety over how to pay the medical bills. The cost of one doctor visit was a staggering eight-hundred dollars, and I saw the doctor daily for six weeks.

I'd become very protective of my eyes and skittish about anything coming near them. I needed Valium just to be coaxed into the examining chair. When the doctor came toward me with tweezers, I recoiled in terror and practically had to be held down. I soaked the chair with perspiration during each doctor visit and I literally shook with fear at the thought of him touching my eyes. So you can understand my reaction when the surgeon announced that he needed to cut my cornea, lift it, and clean under it. I told him, "I'd rather have my legs amputated!"

They say courage is fear that's said its prayers. I learned that truth by experience. I knew there were many people praying for me, my home church as well as churches across the country and even around the globe. I too prayed fervently. I begged God, not only for healing of my eyes, but for strength to endure whatever happened. I had to put my trust in Him, because He was in control and He was the only one who could help me.

While lying awake one night, I clicked on the TV. An all-night station played gentle music as a man read soothing Bible passages. It comforted and calmed me, so I began looking forward to listening every night. I was awake anyway, and it helped the hours pass more quickly.

Like a fountain of fresh water, God's Word, combined with the soothing music, rinsed away my anxiety and worries and replaced them with peace. I was reminded of the words of Jesus: *"Peace I leave with you; my peace I give to you . . . Do not let your hearts be troubled and do not be afraid."* (John 14:27) At last, I was able to say, "Whatever you want, God."

I gave my fears to God and determined to believe in His love for me. I knew He would keep His hand on me, no matter what happened. And I knew He wanted only what was best for me, so why should I fear? If He chose to heal me, I would be unspeakably grateful. If He chose not to, I would remember that He had a reason for that, too. No matter what, with His help, I could go on with my life and use it for Him.

The surgery went well; in time my eyes healed, and my world grew brighter. The pain subsided, and the blackness gradually became a white fog. It was a long road to recovery, but I defied all odds. Slowly the fog grew clearer. After the ordeal, my doctor confided that he hadn't believed I would ever see again. He told me it was a miracle, but I already knew that.

Actually, God gave me two miracles. He healed my eyes, restoring my sight when doctors believed it was hopeless. And, like a plant bursting forth from a dead seed, faith, hope, and trust had blossomed from my fear. Perhaps that was an even greater miracle.

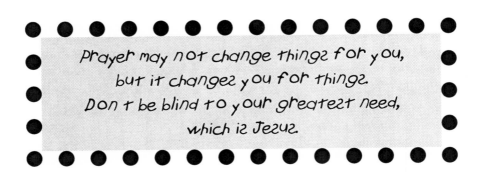

Prayer may not change things for you, but it changes you for things. Don't be blind to your greatest need, which is Jesus.

PANIC ROOM

Have you ever wished, during some horrible time of your life, that you could run into a safe place and hide from the sadness or fear that stalks you? I saw a movie about a mother and daughter whose home was broken into. They hid in a special safe room that nobody could enter from the outside. They called it the panic room.

Everyone needs a place where we feel safe, and I have found such a refuge. It's in the arms of God. Deuteronomy 33:27 says *"The eternal God is your refuge, and underneath are the everlasting arms."* It's comforting to picture God's arms outstretched, ready to catch me if I fall. Psalm 91:2 says *"He is my refuge and my fortress."* A fortress provides strong protection. When the God of the universe is my fortress, I can have courage, even in the midst of fear. David, the shepherd boy turned king, wrote many psalms while fleeing from his enemy, King Saul. At one point, David hid in a cave to escape Saul's wrath.

I understand the fear of being pursued, whether by physical illness, financial troubles, or just an unknown future. I know too well, as David knew, that God doesn't necessarily remove the difficulty. I often wish He would whisk me away to safety. I plead for Him to stop the pain and eliminate the struggle, but the difficulty remains and I must take refuge in God's love, just as David did. While hiding in that cave, David said, *"I will take refuge in the shadow of your wings until the disaster has passed."* (Psalm 57:1 NIV)

God's protection can be compared to that of a mother hen with her chicks. Matthew 23:37 says that God longs to cover us with His wings. Maybe you've heard the story about the hen who gathered her babies under her wings during a fire. When the flames were extinguished, the hen was dead; but her chicks had been spared by the protection of her wings.

Like that mother hen, God sacrificed to save me, not from physical suffering, but from a worse sort of torture—eternal separation from Him.

I don't have a panic room in my house, but I do have one in my heart. I can take refuge from the burdens of life in the mighty fortress that is God.

"Taste and see that the LORD is good; blessed is the man who takes refuge in him." (Psalm 34:8)

No matter how bad things appear, under the protection of God's wings, I'm safe. It's a place not of painlessness, but of comfort and hope.

He keeps his faithful ones hidden in the palm of his hand. (Isaiah 49:2 CEV) There's no place I'd rather be. And I pray that His loving hands are enfolding you.

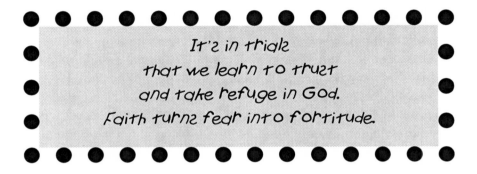

It's in trials
that we learn to trust
and take refuge in God.
Faith turns fear into fortitude.

HUGS, HOPE, AND PEANUT BUTTER

"I know the plans I have for you, declares the Lord. Plans for welfare and not for calamity, and to give you hope and a future." (Jeremiah 29:11)

It all began with a little boy named Michael. Through the Internet, I learned that Michael had a brain tumor. He was the same age as my grandson, who had recently been badly burned. I knew firsthand how helpless a loving adult feels when a little one is suffering and you can't take the pain away. I prayed for Michael and stayed in touch with his family for several months. Meanwhile, through prayer groups, I learned of other sick children who also needed prayers.

I met many desperate parents who found that, in their time of greatest need, friends and family deserted them. They felt isolated, afraid, and forgotten. They were searching for someone who cared enough to help them through the ordeal of watching their child suffer. The mother of one little girl with brain cancer told me she felt like running into the street screaming, "My child is sick! Won't somebody do something?" So I decided to be that somebody. I couldn't do a lot, but I could do something.

A year earlier, due to complications of a connective tissue disease, I'd temporarily lost my eyesight. Though my vision returned, it wasn't clear. Because of scarred corneas, I would forever view the world as if looking through a dirty window. Distinguishing details was difficult, so I was thrown into the world of disability. Because I understood pain, fear, frustration, and isolation, I could relate to and help families affected by illness. Because I could no longer work, I had the time to invest in making a difference for these families. Though my disability seemed at first to be an ending, it became an asset that led to a new beginning. The temporary pause, as my life train switched tracks, propelled me into a new direction.

Michael's family allowed me to put his story on a web page asking visitors to pray for him and send cards to lift his spirits. The cheery mail Michael received from strangers around the country brightened his life. He began to eagerly anticipate each day's mail. It meant a lot to his family that people cared about what they were going through.

Other parents asked to add their children to the web site. They wanted to give their kids something to look forward to besides needles, pain, and sickness. Thus the Hugs and Hope Club for Sick Children was born. Now in its fifth year as a nonprofit charity, the Hugs and Hope Club has one simple goal: to put a little more love, joy, and hope into the lives of sick kids and their families, by sharing God's love and His word with them.

Suffering parents may know in their heads that God cares; but during struggles, they need a real live person "with skin on" to show that love to them. That's what the volunteer hug-givers and hope restorers do. They send hundreds of packages of happy mail to "club kids," including Bible storybooks and beanie bears. They also provide much needed moral support to moms and dads through various programs such as the Parent Pals Project. And any family who requests it receives a free Bible.

In the Hugs and Hope online chat discussion, parents voice their fears, frustrations, and questions. In return, they receive information, support, and encouragement from volunteers and other parents in similar situations. Many close friendships develop in this group.

Over the years, hundreds of children have been part of the club. Children like Nathan and his little brother PJ have benefitted from being part of the group. They suffered from the fatal Batten's Disease and their parents needed one-hundred thousand dollars to pay for medical treatments. Volunteer musicians held a huge benefit, which raised money for the family. As a result of other volunteers contacting television producers, the boys were featured on the show 48 Hours.

Mikey S. was a three year old Leukemia victim. While Mikey was gravely ill, his dad took several days off work to stay with his son in the Intensive Care Unit. Consequently, he lost his job. Volunteers around his state, who had read about Mikey on the Hugs and Hope web site, organized a benefit. Strangers rallied to help the family raise thousands of dollars.

Hunter, another three-year old, lost a kidney to cancer. Volunteers across the nation mailed handmade quilts, afghans, and other items to Hunter's home town in Wisconsin for a raffle. The fundraiser was organized entirely by people who had never even met Hunter.

After his bone marrow transplant, ten-year-old Zack had been in isolation for several weeks. His greatest wish was to meet his favorite rock star. Hugs and Hope volunteers arranged for the singer to not only call the boy, but to send him his own autographed guitar. Zack's smile when he received that guitar is something I won't forget—especially since we were able to grant his wish just weeks before his death. It's heartwarming to know our efforts helped make a child's last days happier.

Although disability closed many doors in my life, God opened a big window and allowed me to be part of more than I had ever imagined. Disability doesn't have to mean you can't accomplish anything worthwhile. With God's guidance, you can do the most worthwhile work of your life.

I've learned to focus on what I can do, rather than on what I can't.

It's funny how God calls us (and enables us) to do things we wouldn't think of on our own. I'm amazed that He would entrust me with running a national nonprofit organization from my living room! I would never have dreamed that I would do such a thing.

I'm an ordinary person with no special talents, yet God allows me to convey His message of love to not only sick children and their families, but to everyone who is touched by HUGS and HOPE. I'm grateful to be part of His work.

Parents tell me this group's encouragement is an invaluable gift. Volunteers say they are blessed by helping. I feel that I gain as much as the people whose lives I touch, so everyone involved in this project benefits.

Hugs and Hope has taught me valuable lessons. For instance, everyone has problems, but it's best to forget our own troubles and focus on someone else's struggle.

Many Hugs and Hope volunteers suffer with serious illnesses, financial struggles, or family problems. Yet, they look beyond themselves and encourage others. Like me, they've learned that when you take your mind off your own problems and give joy to others, peace and contentment boomerang right back to you. The best way to be uplifted yourself is to bend down and help someone else up.

I've also discovered that God can accomplish tremendous things with our smallest efforts, and He can bring something good out of bad situations. My own meager efforts don't amount to much; but, just as it takes many small drops of water to make the ocean, the cumulative effect of many individuals can make a tremendous difference in our world. In one instance, after I posted the story of a little girl on the Hugs and Hope web site, her medical fund account increased by several thousand dollars.

When The Hugs and Hope Club began, I was praying for one little boy named Michael. Before long, it was twenty children. Now it's hundreds. The Hugs and Hope web site began as one page. It's grown to over two hundred pages. Original efforts included saying a prayer and mailing a card. Today, there are dozens of Hugs and Hope programs and projects to help meet the needs of families in crisis.

Volunteers make pillow cases, blankets, and tote bags for hospitalized children. Some crochet angels to remind the kids that God sends guardian spirits to watch over them. Volunteers send get well balloons, birthday party boxes, Christmas ornaments, stockings, and gifts.

I hope that through the Hugs and Hope Club, hurting people will come to know the love and peace available to those who seek and serve God. The Hugs and Hope message is that no one must face struggles alone. God cares about our pain and desires to be intimately involved in each life. He delights in helping us through trials.

Are you good at writing encouraging notes? Do you excel at organizing projects or creating web page graphics? Even if you can do nothing more than mail a Veggie Tales video to a hospitalized child or pray for him, it makes a difference. You can be a part of influencing our world for good. And when you share God's love and give of yourself, He gives you back more than you give. Love, hope, and happiness are like sticky peanut butter. When you spread them around, you can't help but get a whole lot on yourself, too!

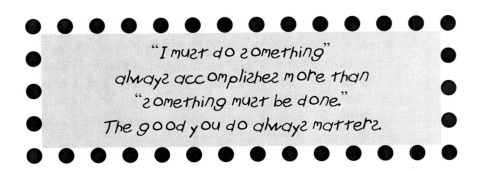

"I must do something"
always accomplishes more than
"something must be done."
The good you do always matters.

Peanut Butter by Bronson M.

Happy mail by Caleb L

RECESS BOO BOO'S

My grandson started kindergarten this week. It's always tough when a distant dream becomes a frightening reality. The adjustment has been difficult. The first day was long and filled with anxiety. There was great apprehension, much fear and worrying, and a whole lot of sobbing . . . but I survived. The second day was a little easier for me; but my son, who is a stay-at-home dad, was a nervous wreck.

We hate to see our little sweetie grow up and go out into the big, bad world all alone. Why do kids begin school at such a tender age, anyway? Five is so young. They should wait until at least twelve. I see these little cherubs walking to school and I wonder, "How can their mothers let them go outside alone?"

I'm a little overprotective, I guess. I don't understand why grandma can't ride the bus with him and sit next to him in school, for the first month at least. No one can protect my sweet potato like his she-bear grammie. Who will kiss his boo-boos if he falls down? Who will yell at the naughty kids who teach him bad words? Who will threaten the bullies who pick on him? Who will see that the teacher gives him the extra special attention that he deserves?

That first day, my imagination was enough to fuel my worries, but then I learned that Cobi had been beat up during recess! This is one of the worst things a grandmother can hear. (I had hoped that my biggest shock the first week of school would be hearing that he'd called the teacher a doo-doo head or a stinky face.) I should have had the foresight to pay off the playground monitor so she'd watch out for him.

It seems that my brave little man tried to rescue a first grade girl who was being harassed by an older boy. When Cobi defended her, the bigger boy knocked him down and gave him a bloody nose. Of course, grandma wanted to go to school and give that bully what for, visit his parents, and call the principal; but my grandson assured me that it wasn't a big deal. In fact, he seemed unbothered by the entire incident.

When I asked what happened after the boy punched him, Cobi casually explained that he hadn't hit back because he "didn't want to hurt the big kid." Grandma couldn't help but smile at that. If you're a parent or grandparent, you probably feel as I do . . . it's harder to deal with adversities affecting our kids than it is facing things that hurt us personally. Don't you wish we could just wrap them in bubble wrap to protect them when they're away from us?

Cobi is speeding toward adulthood faster than a computer virus spreads across the web. He recently took the training wheels off his bike. He's growing up! Before I know it, he'll be driving the car, having children of his own, and visiting me in the old fogies' home. (At least I hope he'll visit.)

I hope that time won't come too soon. There are too many fun things we need to do together before that happens. I plan to savor every one of them. The Bible verse is true that says, *"Children are gifts from God. They are his reward."* (Psalm 127:3)

We may not know what's happening to our kids
when they're out of our sight;
but we are never out of the sight
of our heavenly Father.
He always knows what's happening to us.
He enfolds us in His love,
which is even better than bubble wrap.

Cancer Kids are Special by Ashleigh S.

MY DAY IN THE E.R.

I was driving home from church one snowy Sunday when my van skidded on a patch of ice and overturned. As the ambulance transported me to the hospital, police phoned the husband to notify him.

I lay in the emergency room eagerly waiting for him to come. "What could be keeping him?" I asked the nurse.

"Well, the police said they can't reach him," she explained.

"But I know he's home," I told her. "He wasn't planning to leave the house today. He's working on his boat."

"I need to check on your x-rays," she said, walking to the door. "I'll see if there is any news on your husband too."

When she came back, she told me, "The police are still trying to reach him. They've called several times but they got no answer. They even went to your house, but nobody came to the door when they knocked. They did talk to your neighbor, though. He said he'd go into your house, find your husband, and let him know you're here."

I fumed for hours until that evening when the husband finally arrived. I was more than a little perturbed.

"Where in the world have you been?" I demanded.

"I was in the basement all day," was his innocent reply.

"Weren't you curious about why I didn't come home from church this morning?" I asked through clenched teeth.

"I was busy and didn't notice the time," he said. "I thought you were just on an all-day shopping marathon."

My temper was ready to blow like a bald tire on a Volkswagon bus. "Why didn't you answer the door or the phone?" I snapped.

"I didn't hear them," he said defensively. "The neighbor didn't come over and give me the message till five o'clock."

"Five o'clock?" I shrieked. "It's seven thirty now! What took you so long to get here?"

He winced as if he knew his answer wasn't going to please me. Then he stammered, "Well . . . I had to . . . stop . . . at the junk yard to see the damage to the car."

Lucky for him I was restrained by a back brace. If I hadn't been strapped to the table, he might have needed emergency surgery—to remove my purse from his forehead.

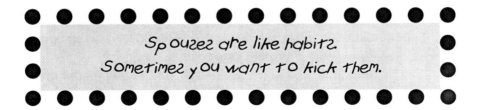

Spouses are like habits.
Sometimes you want to kick them.

HUNKY MAGOO

Hunky Magoo is a fitting nickname for the husband. It's unusual and so is he. I call him "H.M." He likes to think it stands for "His Majesty." H.M. sometimes gives the impression of being unfriendly, but deep down in his heart, he's really anti-social.

Like all men, he has his little idiosyncrasies. For one thing, he's a pack rat. I haven't been able to park my van in our three car garage for ten years because it's overflowing with all the junk he's collected. He hangs onto everything he's ever owned, including the wing tip shoes he bought for our wedding thirty years ago. I can't sneak them out of the house, because he routinely checks the garbage to see if I've thrown away any of his stuff. He thinks the groovy polyester pants he wore in the seventies still have a few good years in them. I've even caught him wearing my cleaning rags.

Hunky's the most handsome, thoughtful, charming husband in the universe—in his opinion. He brags that he can do the work of three men, and it's true, if the three men are Larry, Moe, and Curly. He also brags about having a mind like a steel trap. I tell him he's right about that, because nothing can penetrate it. I also tell him the trap must be stuck, because he keeps forgetting who's the boss around here.

H.M.'s perspective is very different from mine. For instance, he doesn't feel as strongly as I do about things like empty toilet paper rolls. Then there's the issue of dirty underwear. He seems to believe they belong on the bathroom floor. Every morning, I pick them up, along with enough back hair to fill a trash bag. (I'm saving it to weave a rug).

He also has some odd ideas about home decorating. Once, we were to show our house to prospective buyers on a day I had to work. That left H.M. in charge of giving the tour. That morning, I ran through the house giving it a quick inspection. Everything looked good. I grabbed the dirty laundry from the bedroom, ran downstairs, and dropped it into the washer before going out the door.

When I came home that night, the couple was just leaving. I met them on the front porch, thanked them for coming, and went inside to ask the husband how the showing went.

As I stepped through the door, I saw them! There, on the stairs leading up to our bedroom—on the third step to be exact—was a pair of my holey, white, cotton, "grandma" underwear.

At that moment, I can't be sure, but I think I had a stroke. I could almost hear those ragged old bloomers screaming, "Look at me! Look at me!" They mocked me, saying, " Nya, Nya! I've been here all day, right out in the open for all the world to see, and there wasn't a darn thing you could do about it!"

I was mortified. It was the second most embarrassing event of my life. The first most embarrassing was in second grade when my mother gave me a haircut and a poodle perm the day before class pictures were taken. That horrific memory of those tight, one-quar-ter-inch, fuzzy curls and the huge red bow on top of my head, was captured on film to be ridiculed forever by future generations.

Anyway, after my stroke, I got up off the floor, turned to the husband, and groaned, "Please tell me these were not here when the couple walked through the house."

"Yeah, they were," he answered, with the same casual tone he would use to say, "Nice weather we're having, ha?"

I felt a second stroke coming on. An inferno of anger was ris-ing from the pit of my stomach and felt as if it would shoot out my ears. Yet, I made a valiant attempt to control myself. I spoke as calmly as I could. "Tell me," I said quietly. Then, a little louder, I asked, "Why would you leave them there?" Finally, I yelled, "Why didn't you pick them up?"

Looking at me as if I were Quasimodo's ugly cousin from Neptune, he sighed and said, "I didn't want to call attention to them, that's why!"

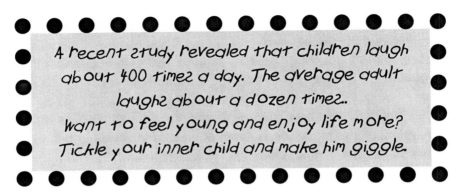

A recent study revealed that children laugh about 400 times a day. The average adult laughs about a dozen times. Want to feel young and enjoy life more? Tickle your inner child and make him giggle.

MY NEXT HUSBAND WILL BE NORMAL

My friend gave me a plaque that read, "My next husband will be normal." I didn't realize how fitting it was until the morning I announced to the husband, "I'm taking a quick bike ride before breakfast. I should be back in half an hour or so." He nodded, heading toward the garage to tear apart a motorcycle.

For a moment, I hesitated—wondering if I should skip my morning ride. I had a migraine and my fibromyalgia and arthritis were acting up too, making it tough for me to even walk. But I was determined not to let my connective tissue disease get the better of me. I was not about to give in to pain and alter my daily schedule of walking, biking, and aerobics class.

After pedaling only about a mile down a deserted sand road, the strength began to drain from my body like air leaking from a balloon. I felt weak, like the energizer bunny without batteries. My ears started ringing and things around me appeared to sprout black fuzz around the edges. My legs went limp like cooked linguini and my body folded up like a cheap lawn chair. Things got blurrier then went totally black.

I awoke in the ditch to the smell of mud and the weight of the heavy bike across my chest. My head and ankle were throbbing.

Bits of gravel were embedded in my skinned palms. When I tried to sit up, the world began to spin again and I felt like I would hurl; so I lay back down in the dirt.

Since I couldn't make it home on my own power, I had no choice but to wait for someone to happen along and help me. Knowing there was rarely any traffic on that road, I clung to the hope that the husband would come to my rescue. *He'll be along any minute*, I reassured myself. *He'll know something's wrong when I'm not back home at the usual time.*

I assumed that when he realized I'd been gone too long, he would wonder if something happened and he'd come looking for me. I was wrong.

I continued to lie there in a rain puddle with rocks and a discarded Pepsi can digging into my back. I felt flaccid like a marionette without strings. Each time I started to stand up, I felt faint, so I spent a good part of the morning lying there at the side of the road.

I pulled grass and a cigarette butt from my hair and spit the sandy grit from between my teeth while watching dead leaves, gum wrappers and other litter blow past me. When a McDonald's bag tumbled by, I wondered who had eaten their Big Mac here, in the middle of nowhere, and then recklessly thrown the trash out their car window.

After a while, the local bugs discovered me. Bees buzzed around my head, ants crawled up my shorts, and Japanese beetles tickled my thighs. Meanwhile, the sun grew hotter as it rose higher in the sky.

I lay there for what seemed like eighteen hours, and I didn't have on my 18-hour bra!

After a while, I finally felt my strength returning. By this time, I had become painfully aware that the husband was not searching for me. Giving up any hope that my knight on horseback was coming to help, I muttered to myself, "If I want to get home before the winter snows come, it's up to me to get myself there."

Using the bike for leverage, I pulled my woozy body up on quivering legs. I couldn't tell if it was the world spinning or just me wobbling. Half standing and half slumping over the handlebars for support, I trudged home. All the way, I mentally rehearsed what I would say to Sir Galahad when I got there.

Staggering into the front yard, I heard cheerful whistling coming from the garage. For a moment I forgot the ringing in my head and the pain in my ankle. I dragged myself toward the whistling and shouted weakly, "I passed out in the road and waited for you to come looking for me!" The husband looked up from his project in surprise, but he said nothing.

"Weren't you worried about what had happened to me when I didn't come right back?"

"I didn't notice that you were gone that long," he replied.

"I was gone half of the day!" I yelped. He stared at me with a puzzled look.

"I could have been killed, flattened by a moving van or a beer delivery truck!" I told him. By this time, I was angry enough to spit hammers; but he still just stood there, silent. I wondered if, while I was gone, he'd been zapped by a lightening bolt and struck dumb. He wiped his hands on a greasy rag and shrugged, as if he couldn't understand what I was upset about.

"My inward parts could have been spilling out all over the road," I ranted, "I could have been devoured by wolves, weasels, or wild cats!" He just scratched his head.

"My eyes could have been plucked out by vultures, coyotes, and hungry arachnids!

All sorts of vermin could have been feasting on my flesh . . . but you didn't even miss me!"

"Sorry," he said, almost in a whisper. He sighed, turned around, and started back toward the garage. Suddenly, he stopped and looked back. I waited expectantly for some delayed display of sympathy.

"Oh," he said, "let me know when lunch is ready."

I was too weak to choke him, but as I fell in a heap on the front porch step, I made this resolution: If I should ever have a next husband, I will definitely attempt to find one that's normal—if that's even possible.

Wait a minute. Maybe this sort of behavior IS normal (for a husband). I hadn't thought of that!

Thank God that this kind of thing is definitely not normal for Him. He is not oblivious to what's happening with me. The psalmist wrote, *"The Lord will watch over your coming and going both now and forever."* (Psalm 121:8) God's never so distracted that He forgets or forsakes me (Deuteronomy 31:6).

When I wander away from Him, He comes looking for me. *"For the eyes of the LORD range throughout the earth to strengthen those whose hearts are fully committed to him."* (2 Chronicles 16:9 NIV)

God's a seeker. In the Bible, He compares himself to a shepherd who is searching for his lost sheep. He doesn't say, "I'm here for you if you want me," or "You want to do things your own way and screw up your life? Then I'll just forget about you!" No, He yearns for time with the children He created and loves. He longs for fellowship. He's always watching and listening for us. Like the hotel commercial, He leaves the light on, hoping we'll come. But He doesn't stop there. He cares enough to come after us. He does everything He can to draw us to Himself. He misses us when we wander away.

"The eyes of the Lord are toward the righteous and His ears are open to their cry." (Psalm 51:16, 17)

God's searching for you, listening for you to call on Him. Will you make Him wait?

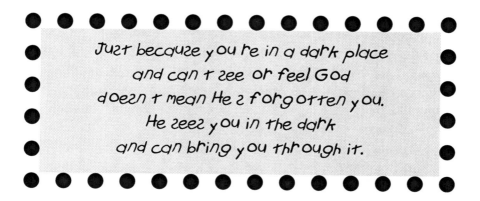

Just because you're in a dark place and can't see or feel God doesn't mean He's forgotten you. He sees you in the dark and can bring you through it.

THIEVES, MURDERERS, AND DONKEYS

Do you feel like you're not important enough, smart enough, or eloquent enough to accomplish something worthwhile? Think again. I used to feel that way, but God showed me I was wrong. He has a purpose for every life and He works through and uses ALL sorts of people. If you're not convinced, consider the following criminals who became great religious leaders:

Moses killed an Egyptian with his bare hands. That's first degree murder. Yet, he later became one of the greatest leaders of God's people.

King David didn't hold the weapon that killed his trusted servant, but he deliberately put Uriah in the line of fire, knowing that he would be killed. David had a thing for Uriah's wife and wanted her husband out of the way. So this wife-stealing king was guilty of premeditated murder and adultery, yet the Bible calls David "a man after God's own heart." Though David messed up big time and failed to do God's will, he valued God's word above all else. He studied it and thought about it continually. This is why God called David His friend.

Joseph had a prison record as a sex offender, but he became second in command to the King of Egypt, thanks to God.

Rahab was a prostitute, but God used her. She hid some of God's people in her house to protect them and her kindness was recorded in the Bible for future generations to read.

The apostle Peter, who had bragged that he would die for Jesus, turned out to be a coward who caved in to peer pressure. Peter denied three times that he even knew Jesus. However, after he repented, he went on to become a great leader in the Christian church.

Paul was a violent man who tortured and killed many Christians before being converted himself to Christianity. This murderer turned preacher started many Christian churches throughout the world and he wrote a good portion of the New Testament.

All twelve disciples chosen by Jesus were lowly, uneducated men. Some were fishermen and one was even a tax collector, considered the lowest of the low. Tax collectors were despised by everyone and considered greedy thieves. Yet Matthew, the tax collector, became one of Jesus' closest friends and one of those who went into the whole world to teach about Him. No matter what you are now or have previously been, God can transform you into what He wants you to be. Even if you have a dark past, your future can be bright. If you lack talent, education, influence, power, money, or good looks, God still has a purpose that only YOU can fulfill in His plan.

In the Old Testament story of Baalam and his donkey, God used an animal to relay his message to a man. If He could use that jack ass, He most certainly can work through you and me too.

But for God to work in and through us, we must surrender and give Him all our problems, regrets, fears, and hurts. We need to put Him in the driver's seat and take our own hands off the wheel. Nothing under God's control can be out of control.

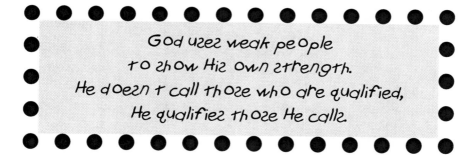

God uses weak people
to show His own strength.
He doesn't call those who are qualified,
He qualifies those He calls.

ANGEL HUGS

Ever wonder what angels look like? Are they gray-haired women with dangling earrings like Della Reese in the television show? Or do they resemble chubby, winged babies portrayed in paintings? I've never seen a spiritual being, so I can't say for sure, but I have encountered some "earth" angels who are just as beautiful as any heavenly spirit could be.

There's my friend Eileen in Illinois who tirelessly keeps records of hundreds of sick children, sending out weekly updates on their status to a network of volunteers across the country. After working all day and caring for her family, Eileen creates beautiful blankets which raise money for toys sent to homebound children. Eileen may not have wings, but she's an angel in my eyes.

Across the country, on the East coast, a forty-something pre-school teacher, Jan, shares the strength and wisdom she gleaned from her battle with cancer. Understanding the terror of facing this disease and the joy of defeating it, Jan helps others wage their own wars. She gathers them under her wings and upholds them, traveling alongside them on their journeys. A gifted graphic artist, Jan also designs web art for sick children. Maybe she's not a real angel, but to those hungering for a listening ear and a hand to hold, Jan is a gift sent from heaven.

In Oklahoma, there's Fred, a quadriplegic who spends many hours each day typing uplifting messages to lighten hearts and restore hope to those weary of life's struggles. It's the tapping of a computer keyboard I hear, but it sounds strangely like the fluttering of angel wings.

Autumn, in Idaho, packs a lot of love into each box of goodies she mails to hospitalized children. She boasts no supernatural powers, but the smiles she provides are nothing short of miraculous.

In Florida, Cathie moderates a chat group which is really a lifeline for weary parents to find encouragement, bask in acceptance and understanding, and make lasting friendships. Though she has no halo, Cathie is an angel to hundreds of chatters who depend upon her technical skills.

In New Jersey, Terresa, a busy mom of two little girls, organizes fundraisers which pay for beanie bears, balloon bouquets, and books for sick kids who look forward to receiving "happy mail."

These heavenly folks are just a few of the twenty-five hundred plus members of the Hugs and Hope Club—a group of the most caring, selfless angels this side of heaven. They are ordinary people, linked by the Internet, who are accomplishing extraordinary things through their combined efforts. The club is seeking more hope-restoring earth angels to join them in spreading love (and a little heaven on earth) to sick kids and their families—one smile at a time. To become a Hugs and Hope angel, all you need is a caring heart and the desire to share your love. To learn more, visit the Hugs and Hope web site at www.hugsandhope.org.

Angel by Karissa

To ease another's heartache
is to forget your own.
(Abe Lincoln)

NIGHT SOUNDS

Cobi is five years old. Like most kids his age, he doesn't understand the reasoning behind going to sleep when he still has energy left and there are still hours in the day. One night I was unusually tired and eager to get some sleep, but Cobi was wide awake and resisting sleep with all his power.

He used every excuse he could think of to stay up. He needed a drink, then he needed to go to the bathroom, then he needed a particular stuffed animal that he'd left downstairs. After finally getting him tucked in, I went to brush my teeth.

Over the sound of the water running, I heard him call, "Gra-a-a-a-a-a-ma."

"What's wrong?" I called back.

"I'm too hot. Can I change into different pajamas?"

"All right," I agreed. We found some light weight summer PJs with a big "S" on the chest. Of course, that meant he had to fly around the room a few times before leaping back into bed in a single bound. I kissed him goodnight for the second time and turned off the light.

While putting my night gown on in the other room, I heard, "Gra-a-a-a-a-a-ma."

I went to see what the problem was. "My back is itchy, can you scratch it?" I scratched it. Then I tucked him in again and left the room.

Before I got to the end of the hall, I heard, "Gra-a-a-a-a-a-ma." This time, we had to check the closet for monsters. After finding the coast clear, I pretended to lock the closet door and throw away the key. "Even if there were monsters in there, " I said, "they couldn't get out now."

A minute or two after I left his room, again came the familiar call, "Gra-a-a-a-a-a-ma." He was still too hot, so we opened a window and threw back one blanket. "How's that?" I asked with a yawn. "That's good," he said, "but I'm hungry." Even though he'd had a snack before the bedtime ritual began, how could I send a starving child to bed? I'm a grandma, so what could I say? After a banana and a slice of cheese, I tucked him in *again*.

He was quiet for a good three minutes, but then he needed to get up and blow his nose. And then he needed his pillow fluffed up. And then he remembered that he hadn't hugged grandpa goodnight, so downstairs we went to do that. As I was tucking him in that time, he announced that he was thirsty from the salty cheese.

"Now Cobi," I said, fighting to keep my eyes open, "You can have one more drink and that's it. I'm very sleepy. I can't stay awake any longer. I need to go to sleep and so do you. If you call grandma any more, I'm going to be upset."

He sighed, curled up beneath the blanket, and said, "Okay, grandma."

Exhausted and ready for a good night's sleep, I fell into my bed. Then I heard a timid little voice from down the hall calling "Mar-r-r-r-r-r-sha."

Kids resist sleep because they have a passion for life and they want to squeeze every drop of enjoyment out of each day. Their philosophy is "Play hard, laugh lots, and let your father do the worrying." They have the right idea. We should strive to be innocent and trusting like kids are . . . and leave the worrying to our father too.

"*He (Jesus) called a little child and had him stand among them.*" He said: "*I tell you the truth, unless you change and become like little children, you will never enter the kingdom of heaven.*" (Matthew 18:2,3)

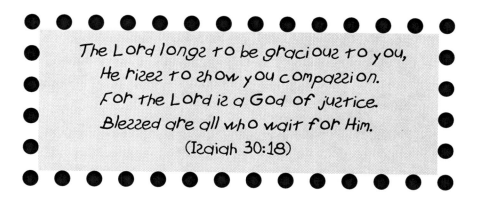

The Lord longs to be gracious to you,
He rises to show you compassion.
For the Lord is a God of justice.
Blessed are all who wait for Him.
(Isaiah 30:18)

A WOMAN'S PREROGATIVE

Being an indecisive person, I tend to go back and forth—never quite sure of my decisions. I'm afraid of making the wrong choice, so quite often I procrastinate in making any decision at all. We women have a reputation for changing our minds.

David, the writer of many Psalms in the Bible, changed his mind a lot too. Like me, he was sort of moody. (But he couldn't use PMS as an excuse!) The psalms illustrate the various emotions David felt.

In Psalm 22, he goes from complaining about his situation to thanking and trusting God. I think this must be typical human behavior. One minute we are confident and trusting, but the next minute we're fearful. Even people with great faith falter at times and doubt.

The good news is that even if we change, God never changes. He is always loving, always trustworthy, always compassionate, always merciful, always forgiving.

"The steadfast love of the Lord never ceases. His mercies never come to an end." (Lamentations 3:23)

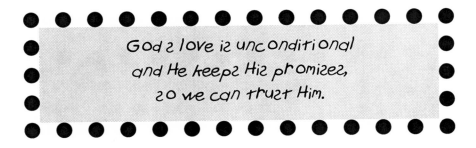

God's love is unconditional
and He keeps His promises,
so we can trust Him.

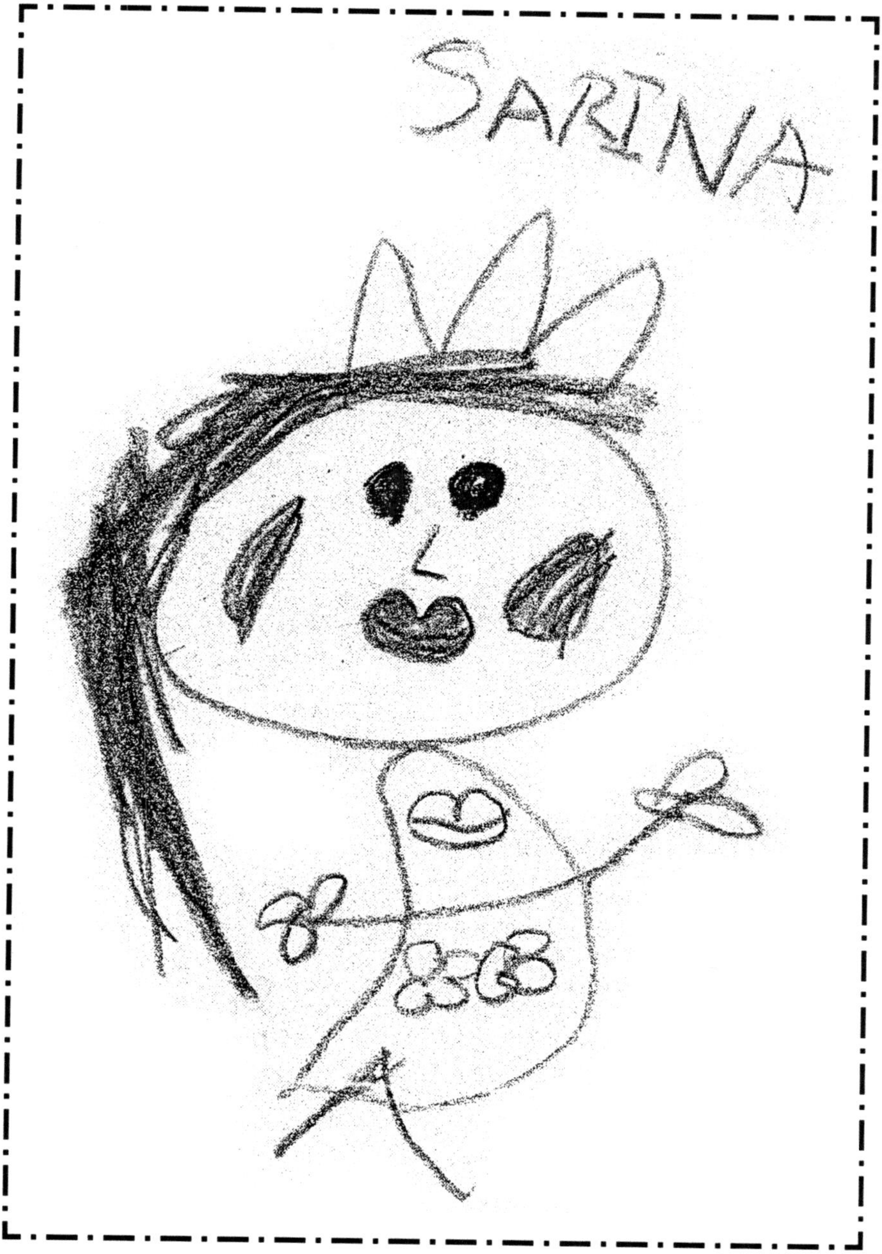
SARINA

Happy Girl by Sarina S.

CHAPTER TWO

LOOKING UP

Bibles that are falling apart
usually belong to people who are not.

WHAT'S MY LINE?

Remember that old TV show where contestants questioned three guests to determine which were impostors and which one was really who they all claimed to be? Sometimes I feel like I'm living in that game show! There are so many sides to me that come out in different circumstances, I wonder which personality is the real me. I can act in ways that go against everything I believe in. I often surprise and disappoint myself, doing things I later regret.

Have you ever wished you could go back in time and do things right? I'm still feeling guilty for the time I was rude my neighbor two years ago. I hate it when I discover personality traits within myself that I detest in other people. I feel at times as if multiple personalities are battling for control of my body. I want to yell, "Will the real Marsha please stand up!"

But if the real me could stand up, would I even like her? Would she be anything like what I think the real me is?

I like to believe that I'm perfect and I certainly want others to believe that I always have the best motives and intentions; but the truth is that no matter how good I try to convince myself or others that I am, I'm imperfect. I goof up and let my selfishness get the best of me when I want what I want when I want it. I forget to think of others, and I run over their feelings like an army tank. When I get frustrated, words come out that astonish me; and I wish I could suck them back in before they reach anyone's ears.

Just who am I really? I may never fully know myself; but God does. And the good news is that He loves me no matter how much I fall short of His desires for me. Of all the things Jesus was called in the Bible, my favorite is "friend of sinners." He said in Matthew 9:13, "For I have not come to call the righteous, but sinners."

It doesn't matter who the real me is. Instead of fretting about that, I'm learning to focus on learning who HE is – the God who not only knows my name, but who has counted the very hairs on my head.

My happy family by Colton M.

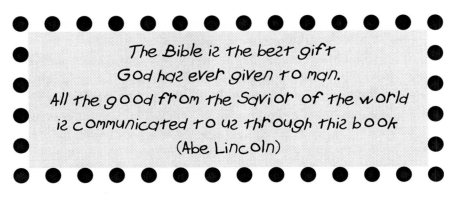

The Bible is the best gift
God has ever given to man.
All the good from the Savior of the world
is communicated to us through this book
(Abe Lincoln)

STORM DEBRIS

After some friends lost their home in a tornado, I helped them clean up what was left. There wasn't much. Where their house had once stood was a refrigerator. That's all. Destruction was everywhere. Debris covered the yard and the nearby woods. All day we sorted through the rubble, hoping to find intact some piece of our friends' lives. We could rescue only a few belongings. We uncovered some important papers, a few small personal items, and a handful of photos—not very much to represent an entire lifetime. I'm sure the family treasures these mementos because they're all that remains from their pre-tornado life.

Like the devastating winds of a tornado, I've felt trouble beat against my life. Hardships blow into every life, threatening to knock down all that we value. In the wreckage, we can usually find some valuable treasures, if our eyes are open to recognize them and our hearts are open to receive them.

"*As long as we're in this world, we will have tribulation*" (John 16:33). But this Bible verse also says, "*In me you may have peace.*" How can we have peace amid tribulation? Peace doesn't result from the removal of unpleasant circumstances. It comes from releasing our own plans and being open to God's plan. Rest comes from fixing our eyes on Him instead of on circumstances. It comes from giving up on living for myself and living for Him instead.

From God's vantage point, there is no true debris. I'm confident that He is in the midst of any storm, and I try to keep my eyes open to see the gift He gives with the rubble. He has promised that, for those who love Him, He'll bring blessings out of storms.

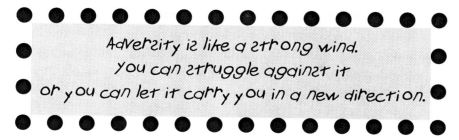

Adversity is like a strong wind.
You can struggle against it
or you can let it carry you in a new direction.

UNSOLVED MYSTERIES

The husband has a favorite TV show. It's whatever happens to be on the History Channel when he's in the mood to veg out on the couch. He also likes to watch "Unsolved Mysteries." I don't watch that show with him, though. I'm too busy trying to solve my own mysteries.

One show I do like is the one about cold case files. You know, where investigators solve a crime thirty years after some poor innocent sap has gone to the electric chair for it. I enjoy watching guilty culprits get caught red handed. I just wish I could see that sort of justice in my own home.

Things around my house keep disappearing. The husband noticed it too, but he blames me and insists that I "steal" his paper work, his glasses, and his tools. He stomps around the house demanding where I've hidden them. Why would I take (or hide) his stuff, for heaven's sake? I don't have time for such nonsense. I'm too busy searching for my own stuff that he has hidden.

Or could it be our son taking things, in an attempt to drive us crazy so we'll be committed? Maybe he wants to inherit the weed whacker and our van.

Perhaps I'm too quick to blame the family. Perhaps it's somebody (or some thing) else sneaking into the house wreaking havoc. But who would steal our socks from the dryer? I have one drawer of matched pairs and six drawers overflowing with unmatched singles. How do they disappear? Does the dryer door lead to the twilight zone?

My son thinks the Keebler elves besiege our home while I'm out buying their cookies, along with Cheetos, Hershey bars, Diet

Coke, and Slimfast shakes. I've entertained the possibility that wild banshees lurk under the recyclables in my garage till I leave, and then hold demon fests in the house. That would explain the empty orange juice cartons, sticky blobs of spilled ketchup in the fridge, and those green Kool Aid stains on the bathroom ceiling.

Maybe it's gnomes sneaking in through the basement window, breaking my irreplaceable antique glassware, scattering candy wrappers and old pizza behind the furniture, and sticking already-been-chewed gum to the under side of the dining room table.

I suspect the CIA. I haven't figured out, though, why their covert operations would involve not only our socks, but our remote control and our car keys.

The biggest mystery in my house is who found and ate my secret stash of Mars bars in the back of the cupboard under the dish towels! I don't know if Scotty beamed them up or if I should blame our dog, King Louie. Perhaps I should interrogate our neighbor's suspicious looking toddler.

Other mysteries that I suspect will remain forever unsolved include how an observant husband, who calculates the number of visitors I have each day by the tire tracks in the driveway, could not know how to change a roll of toilet paper. This is a man who constructs skyscrapers, yet he can't put his underwear in the washer, notice an overflowing garbage can, or find his own socks. And why do kids wait till after your spring cleaning to have a laughing contest and squirt tomato soup out their noses onto the cupboards and freshly painted walls?

How can my five year old grandson fix my broken computer and program the VCR when I can't? And why is it that my son never threw up in the car on the WAY to church, but as soon as we were seated in the front row, he coughed up his cookies? How come he waited till the middle of a silent prayer to yell out a string of obscenities to the shocked woman in the row behind us?

I may never figure out why preschoolers feel compelled to tell the fat lady ahead of us in the check out line that she has a huge butt. And I'll never understand why my son flushed a carrot down the toilet and put a wadded up gum wrapper up his nose, but there's a wonderful mystery I can understand. Jesus said, *"To you it has* been given to know the mystery of the kingdom of God." This mystery is that His life bought my ticket so I could be transferred from the kingdom of darkness into His kingdom of light and life.

Thank God that He provided His written word so that, through it, I can more fully know Him and understand the spiritual mysteries He wants to teach me. Though I may never learn how to set that VCR clock, through God's word, I can understand His great love for me and His will for my life.

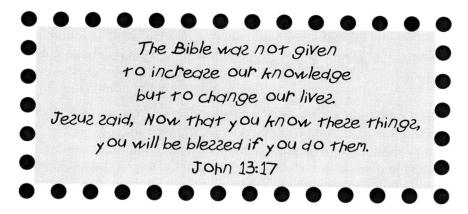

The Bible was not given
to increase our knowledge
but to change our lives.
Jesus said, Now that you know these things,
you will be blessed if you do them.
John 13:17

YOU'RE NOT THE BOSS OF ME!

I laugh when I hear kids say "You're not the boss of me!" Or when they complain, "He's touching me!" Have you ever wondered where kids get these lines? They seem to be universal, so I'm guessing that there must be a special book of one-liners for kids that they all memorize.

The book must contain all the useful lines kids use like "That's not fair," "He did it," and "Make him stop looking at me!" I'm guessing there must be a chapter in the Kid Manual on how to burp and pass gas simultaneously. My grandson is working to master that one.

Is there a book instructing kids on the fine art of gargling the national anthem and how to squirt tomato soup out your nose? Have kids read in this book that they're required to leave every light in the house on and slam the door whenever they leave? I'll bet the book even suggests ideas for relieving boredom—like flushing Mr. Potato Head's body parts down the toilet, counting how many rocks will fit in baby brother's ear, staring into an open refrigerator for hours, or experimenting to see whether a pop tart will fit into (and come out of) the VCR.

Are there chapters in this Kid Book devoted to faking illness to get out of school, hiding your vegetables under the place mat, and how to avoid cleaning up dog barf?

I'm thinking of writing a handbook for moms. I would fill it with lines that every parent needs in their arsenal, such as: *Act your age, I'm not talking just to hear my own voice, there are children starving in China, don't run in the house,* and *your eyes will stick like that.*

Next would come the world-famous questions: *If all the other kids jumped off a cliff, would you do it too?*, *Were you born in a barn? What did I tell you?*, and *Do I look like I'm made of money?*

No book would be complete without *I'll give you something to cry about, I wasn't born yesterday,* and *don't make me stop this car.* Then, of course, there is that timeless classic, *because I said so,* and my personal favorite, *you'll poke your eye out with that*!

Actually, we don't need handbooks to learn these sayings. There's no kid manual to teach the mechanics of making parents crazy. Kids are born knowing that stuff. And there's not a parental hand book listing emergency one liners or instructions on how to nag your kids.

There is, however, an instruction book that's really all any of us need. Because my goal is to be a disciple of Jesus, I study His ultimate instruction book, the Bible. I want to abide in His Word to make GOD the boss of me!

Jesus said we should abide in His word.
(John 8:31)
That means not only read the Bible,
but apply its principles to our lives.
We must become doers of the word
and not hearers only.
(James 1:22)
God's blessings come from obeying.

CUPCAKES, CHEETOS, AND COOKIES, OH MY!

Are you the type of person who eats when you're stressed? I am. I eat when I'm stressed, when I'm sad, when I'm happy, and when I'm tired. I believe there's a food for every mood.

I eat for any reason at any time. I eat when I'm watching television, I eat while riding in the car, and I even eat while sitting at the computer. There are enough crumbs in my keyboard to feed a troupe of boy scouts. Every once in a while, I just shake it over the table and announce to the husband, "Dinner's ready!"

I eat too much, too often. Since I was a kid, I've had a weight problem. I could never "weight" for the next meal. I began wearing a girdle to school in kindergarten, and I've been on diets for most of my life.

I recently began yet another new eating regimen. Forbidden food groups include appetizers and desserts, anything processed or fried, and anything with meat or dairy products in it. I must also avoid all foods seen on TV commercials or restaurant menus. I cannot eat anything prepared by my grandma, Aunt Hildegard, my third cousin twice removed, or any other member of the family. It's called the Oriental Diet. I can eat all I want from the specified food list (celery, kale, bok choi, and those tiny ears of corn), but I must use only one chopstick.

This week, I've failed miserably at sticking to my eating plan. I've had an insatiable appetite for junk food. In addition to a dumpster load of Hostess Twinkies, I've devoured roughly eleven cases of raspberry Fig Newtons and eight and a half pounds of extra crunchy Cheetos. I can't be sneaky about it either. When the husband asks if I've eaten all the Cheetos, how can I look innocent when my fingers and teeth are orange?

Wouldn't you think that after stuffing myself with junk food all week I'd be satisfied? I'm not. In fact, the more I eat, the more I crave. If I continue this way, I'll need a front end loader to lift my carcass out of the Lazy Boy.

To make matters worse, I don't get enough exercise. But I really can't do much that's physical, because I think I pulled a fat cell. I'm barely able to crawl to the kitchen for six square meals a day.

I really need to lose weight. I want to know how it feels to bend over and tie my shoes without cutting off the blood supply above my waist and feeling as if my intestines are being pushed out my ears. It would be great to zip my jeans without fainting from lack of oxygen. So I must get back on track. I'll paste on my refrigerator door that old proverb uttered by some wise sage: "If it tastes good, spit it out."

From now on, I'll plan my meals around a main dish of parsley. Only nutritional foods will pass my lips, like rutabagas, spinach, and celery—stuff that takes half an hour to chew. By the time I swallow them, my aching jaws will be too tired to munch extra-crunchy Cheetos or anything else. Now if I could only figure out a way to make veggies taste like turtle cheesecake.

To keep my weight down and my arteries clean, I must eat health-restoring foods. Similarly, keeping my spiritual arteries open and flowing freely requires health food for my soul. Whoever coined the phrase "Garbage in, garbage out" knew what he was talking about. When I dump into my spirit things that I'm better off without, they transform my perceptions, attitude, and actions. The result can be just as shocking as that horror-filled moment when I view my cellulite-riddled body in Wal-Mart's dressing room mirror.

So, I've made two resolutions. One is to strengthen my body and fuel it with life-sustaining foods. Also, I'll incorporate into my lifestyle more exercise than just aerobic eating and lifting extra large Hershey bars. I'll start slowly with the goal of working up to three sit ups a day. And instead of walking, I'll jog from my bed to the table.

I also plan to exercise my faith and feast spiritually on the word of God. This will be easier and much more palatable than a physical diet; and it will keep my sin-sick, love-starved soul in tip-top health. Bible study is the meat that gives me strength for handling stress and a clear mind to make good decisions. And, unlike Chinese food, it doesn't leave me feeling empty in an hour.

Jeremiah 15:16 says, *"When your words came, I ate them; and they were my joy and my heart's delight."* Jesus promised that whoever hungers and thirsts for righteousness will be satisfied, and Psalm 63:5 testifies, *"My soul will be satisfied as with the richest of foods."*

I feel better already.

Taste and see that the Lord is good.
(Psalm 34:8)

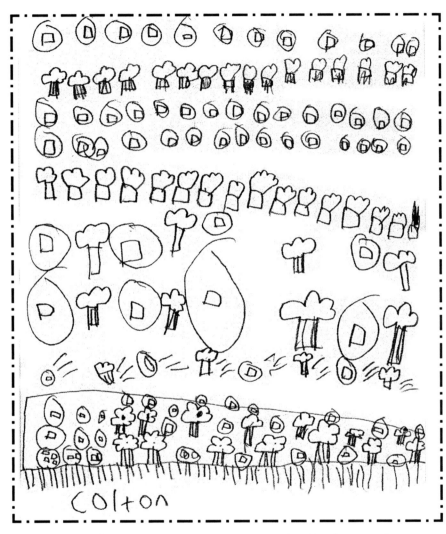

Cookies and cupcakes by Colton M.

TRUE RICHES

Do you know anybody who has won big on the slot machines in Las Vegas? I wouldn't mind having money spill out of a machine into my pockets, but that's not likely to happen since I don't gamble. However, I am rich because I possess a treasure greater than money. It provides great joy, it helps me get to heaven, and it can change my life on earth. It's free and available to anyone. It's a love letter written from the heart of the all-powerful creator of the world. It's the Bible.

If God suddenly appeared before us and wanted to chat, wouldn't we drop everything and pay close attention to what He had to say? Yet, we have a written message from Him and many of us ignore it. We would get excited about meeting the president, famous athletes, or movie stars. Why don't we show the same enthusiasm and awe when we encounter the highest power in the universe through His written word?

Is your Bible hidden away on a shelf? Do you even own one? In some countries, it's illegal to read the Bible. In others, Bibles are so expensive that only the wealthy can afford them. I have five Bibles in my house, but most families around the globe have none; and they'd be grateful for an opportunity just to borrow one periodically.

Do you appreciate the treasure that's sitting on your coffee table collecting dust? Do you take advantage of our freedom to study the wisdom contained in this book?

I don't need to gamble in Vegas for riches. The greatest treasure in this world is available to me wherever I am. It may be as close as my corner bookshelf.

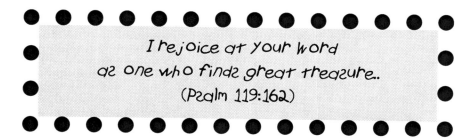

I rejoice at your word
as one who finds great treasure.
(Psalm 119:162)

CAN YOU HEAR ME?

As we age, the hearing and eye sight are usually the first things to go, but my memory beat them to it. My smarts checked out of Hotel Cerebellum long ago.

My four-year-old grandson, frustrated by my poor memory, suggested that I visit a "head doctor." When I asked why, he told me, "You need somebody to help you think smarter because you have a bad brain."

It's sad when a preschooler realizes that he's smarter than you are. The kid's not even in kindergarten and he's outgrown me. I'm reminded of something the Bible says about people who have trouble seeing, hearing and understanding.

"*Therefore I speak to them in parables,*" Jesus said, "*because seeing they do not see, and hearing they do not hear, nor do they understand . . .*" (Matthew 13:13) Why do some people not hear, see, and understand what God tells them? It's not a communication problem. It's a heart problem.

"*For the hearts of this people have grown dull. Their ears are hard of hearing, and their eyes they have closed . . . lest they should understand with their hearts and turn, so that I should heal them.*" (Matthew 13:15) Though God speaks to us through the Bible, we can be slow to understand. Our hearts are not receptive. We have selective hearing.

We all need to open our eyes and ears to see and hear not just what we want to see and hear, but what God is trying to communicate to us!

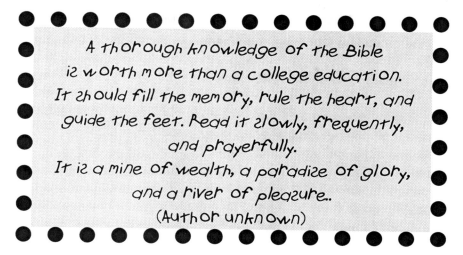

A thorough knowledge of the Bible
is worth more than a college education.
It should fill the memory, rule the heart, and
guide the feet. Read it slowly, frequently,
and prayerfully.
It is a mine of wealth, a paradise of glory,
and a river of pleasure..
(Author unknown)

WHO IS HE, ANYWAY?

There was a time in my life when I wrestled with the question, "Who is this Jesus, anyway?" The Bible book of Acts, which details events that transpired after Jesus died, states *"Salvation is found in no one else, for there is no other name under heaven given to men by which we must be saved."* (Acts of the Apostles 4:12)

That sentence has the potential to start wars. In the first century, those who taught it were tortured and killed, and it continues to stir up opposition today.

Some people believe Jesus was a good man, or a great teacher, or a prophet of God. Which is it? Or was he more than all these? To answer this question, I recently read through the gospel written by John.

What others said about Him:

The book of John tells us that John the Baptist believed Jesus was the "son of God' and "the one from Heaven." The first eighteen verses of the book describe Jesus as the "creator of all things," the "one and only son of God," the one "who existed from the beginning," the one who is "full of truth," and the one who was "with God and was God." Verse 14 says that Jesus "became flesh," indicating that he had existed previously as more than a mere man.

What He claimed about Himself:

Jesus made several claims in his own words regarding who he was. In the third chapter of John, Jesus calls himself "the one who came from heaven" and "God's only Son." In the fourth chapter, he refers to himself as the "gift of God." In chapter six, he stated that he was "the bread of life" that "came from heaven." In chapter eight, he called himself the "light of the world." In chapter ten, he compared himself to the "narrow gate that leads to life" and the "good shepherd." In that chapter, he also stated that he "and the Father are one." In the fourteenth chapter, Jesus described himself as "the way, the truth, and the life," and he said that "No one comes to the Father except through me." He also instructed that everyone should obey whatever he commanded. In chapter fifteen, Jesus compared us to branches that remain alive only by staying connected with him, "the true vine."

In the fourth chapter of John, a woman told Jesus, "*I know that Messiah (called Christ) is coming.*" Jesus told her, "*I am he.*"

In chapter eight, Jesus told the people, "If you do not believe I am the one I claim to be, you will die in your sins." And he told them, "*Abraham rejoiced at the thought of seeing my day. Before Abraham was born, I AM.*" This indicates that Jesus existed eternally.

He told the Jewish people that their scriptures testified about him, yet they did not believe what Moses had written about him. (John 5:39, 40) When the Jews gathered around Jesus (John 10) and asked, "*If you are the Christ, tell us plainly,*" Jesus answered, "*I did tell you, but you do not believe me.*"

The Bible says there is no other name that will cause every knee to bow and every tongue to confess that He is Lord. Jesus was not just another teacher. He was the son of God sent on a mission to teach his brothers about truth and heaven. But more importantly, He was sent to die in order to save us–all of us. Young, old, rich, poor, educated, ignorant. Every one. That means you. He died for you. Are you living for Him? *What a brother!*

Reading the gospel of John gave me a fresh insight into who Jesus is. I hope my attitude will always be like that of the boy in the following story:

To be like Him:

It was the day after Christmas and the man parked his car to pick up the morning paper. He noticed a dirty, poorly dressed boy looking at his car. Seeing the boy eyeing the car, he reminded himself to be quick or he might be missing a hubcap when he returned. He came out of the store with his paper under his arm and just as he opened the door to the car, the boy asked, "Mister, how much would a new car like this cost?" Mr. Greene responded, "I really don't know; my brother gave me this car as a gift." The ragged little boy looked unbelievingly at the car and then, with a look of wonder in his eyes, said, "Gee, I wish I could be a brother like that."

You see, at just the right time, when we were still powerless, Christ died for the ungodly. Very rarely will anyone die for a righteous man, though for a good man someone might possibly dare to die. But God demonstrates His own love for us in this: While we were still sinners, Christ died for us. (Romans 5:6 & 7)

CHAPTER THREE

LEARNING TO TRUST

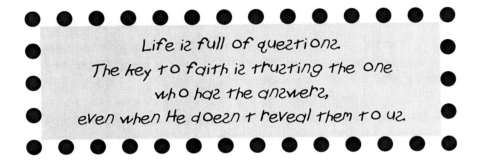

Life is full of questions.
The key to faith is trusting the one
who has the answers,
even when He doesn't reveal them to us.

THE BEAR FACTS

Last night, while I sat near the patio door reading, a hulking black bear lumbered up the steps of the deck behind me. At the railing, he rose on his hind legs. With a swat of one huge paw, he knocked our bird feeder to the ground.

How does a grown woman react when she's standing almost nose to nose with a 200-pound wild animal? First, she thanks God for the thin sheet of glass separating them. Then, she screams like a screech owl for her husband, of course. The husband (who is much braver than I am when a bear is standing three feet away) slid the glass door open and yelled "Get outta here!" But I don't think this bear understood English—or human for that matter.

The bear's lack of fear disturbed me. Now, I'm not the kind of person who strikes fear in any heart, so it was no surprise to me that I didn't scare the bear. The husband, on the other hand, is definitely one scary dude. He looks like a deranged Grizzly Adams, and he could easily win an axe murderer look alike contest. Let me put it this way: If we were strangers and I encountered him on a dimly lit street, I would cross to the other side, step up my pace, and keep my spraying finger planted firmly on the nozzle of my mace can. The only way he could be scarier is if he had big bushy eyebrows and hair growing out his ears and nose. Oh, wait. He already does have big bushy eyebrows and hair growing out his ears and nose. Well, then, I guess the only way he could be any scarier would be if he had three arms, an extra eye in the middle of his forehead, and teeth protruding from his ears.

But back to the bear. He or she—whatever it was (it's difficult to determine a bear's gender without close inspection, which I'm not willing to attempt) —this bear was not afraid of the husband. It ignored him, intent upon gobbling its bird seed snack. Only after it had finished the last sunflower seed and destroyed what was left of the bird feeder, did the bear stroll off into the woods.

For you city folks who may not understand the ways of the woods, let me enlighten you about bears. In the Fall, they stuff themselves silly (much like I do all year long). They gorge themselves with berries, garbage, and dead things (much like my dog does). They develop a huge layer of belly fat (much like mine). Then they sleep for several months (which is an effective way to avoid the cold north woods winters). What a life! I should have been born a bear. I do, after all, have the temperament and hairy legs for it, and I would love to sleep the winter away.

Anyway, bears awake from hibernation with tremendous appetites (kind of like mine after I've fasted for two hours), but there is little for bears to eat in Spring when vegetation hasn't begun to grow.

Now, if a bear's stomach is anything like mine, its middle-of-the-night growling cannot be ignored. In fact, the quiet grumble intensifies till it sounds like a howler monkey screaming "Feed me—NOW!" Many nights, out of necessity, I abandon my cozy bed and forage for food. Hunger compels me to do it. I hate stumbling downstairs in a sleepy fog to search for a midnight snack, usually stubbing a toe or running into a wall along the way. However, my demanding gut is as relentless as a teenager begging for car keys. It keeps annoying, wearing me down, till I can't stand any more and I'll do whatever it takes to appease it.

It's the same way for bears. Their children don't beg for car keys, but their ravenous appetites dictate their behavior. They become more bold and aggressive when food is scarce. That's why I don't take spring-time hikes through the woods. In fact, I'm not real brave in my own front yard.

I often cross the yard between my house and car while unconcerned critters munch away at my lawn, eyeing me with a nonchalant air that implies, "This is OUR territory. Why are YOU in it?"

We've shooed porcupines away more than once for chomping on our porch posts. And there's a mini herd of cavalier deer who dine each evening just steps from my front door.

So you can understand why I'm a little apprehensive outside in the dark. Actually, I'm more than a little apprehensive. I'm a big chicken. That's why I take my dog out with me (all fifteen poodle-pounds of him) to stand guard while I carry groceries in from the car.

King Louie's duty is to scare away monsters, burglars, and beasts, but he's not cut out for the job. He intimidates no one except the fainthearted UPS man who hasn't yet discovered that Louie doesn't have teeth.

Once, a defiant buck had the gall to stroll right onto my porch in pursuit of my pansies. It sniffed at the dumbfounded dog who stood mute, trembling with fear. And I'm no better than Louie at scaring away wild animals. They ignore me, even when I stomp, yell, and flap my flabby arms like a giant, crazed, bat-woman.

The scariest pests are definitely the bears. I don't much like them invading my personal space. When brazen bruins began busting down our bee hives to steal honey, that was the last straw. We kept moving the hives closer to our house until they were finally just outside the back door. Yet, the hungry bears were undaunted. They continued to mosey right up to the house. Each time I opened the door, I expected to find myself face to face with Smokey and his kinfolk.

I was also miffed because, now that the hives were so close, bees were entering the house as often as I did. Keep in mind that thousands of bees live in each hive. That's a lot of stingers. The female bees are the workers. While they're out collecting nectar all day, the male bees do nothing but hang around the hive watching TV, drinking beer, and scratching themselves. All those thousands of drones are brimming with testosterone and looking for a fight. These kings of sting are easily agitated and bored because they don't have much excitement in their lives. Their only entertainment is waiting for some unsuspecting victim to wander near so they can torment him. Okay, I know the rotten little buggers are necessary for pollination and all that, but I hate any critter that has a lethal weapon attached to its rear end. (I'm consoled, however, by the fact that they die immediately after stinging me.)

Cohabitation with angry, stinging bees doesn't bother the husband. His hide, like a thick-skinned bear's, is impenetrable. He doesn't mind being attacked by swarms of the ornery, little dive-bombing lancet launchers. He once received 200 stings in one day. Yet, he still actually likes these disgusting kamikaze bugs. He even catches wild ones (of the bumble variety) to show our grandson. "Go ahead," he tells Cobi, "Pick it up and pet it." This makes grandma faint.

The husband was reluctant to part with his beloved bees, but he wasn't willing to share their honey with mooching bears either. This created a dilemma.

Determined to live in a bee-free, bear-free home, I put my foot down. We discussed the options and then we compromised by doing things my way. We got rid of the bees, the hives, and the honey, which eliminated the bear problem. We learned to get by without honey; but knowing we were outwitted by dumb animals was tougher to live with.

The moral behind all this critter talk is this: Animals that don't fear people don't live long. I think it's safe to say that hunger is hazardous to their health.

This truth applies to humans too. Don't our appetites get us into trouble? I know I'm guilty of sometimes acting like a dumb animal. When I see something I want, I often throw caution to the wind and do foolish things. (For proof of this, check my closet.)

Cravings for clothes, cars, houses, power, money, sex, control, praise, or status can be hazardous to our health—both physical and eternal life.

There's a Bible story of a man who, like a hungry bear, allowed his appetite to affect his judgment. Because he was hungry, Esau made the impulsive decision to forfeit his greatest possession.

Genesis 25:29-34: *When Jacob had cooked stew, Esau came in from the field . . . and Esau said to Jacob, "Please let me have a swallow of that red stuff there, for I am famished." But Jacob said, "First sell me your birthright" . . . so he . . . sold his birthright to Jacob. Then Jacob gave Esau bread and lentil stew, and he ate and drank.*

All I can say is Esau must have been one hungry dude. Lentils wouldn't tempt me a bit. (Chocolate, however, is another story.) Esau was hungry enough to eat even legumes. He abandoned good sense for a bowl of beans, sacrificing his inheritance for instant gratification. I'm tempted to self-righteously say, "Way to go, bright guy!" But I shouldn't be too quick to judge, because I can be just as foolish.

Selfish desires and lack of self-control lead down a destructive path. Philippians 3:18-20 says, *"Many walk . . . that are enemies of the cross of Christ, whose end is destruction, whose God is their appetite . . . who set their minds on earthly things."*

Whoa! These are strong words. How can my appetites (desires) become my gods? Here's how: When I love or desire something more than God, I put it first in my life. I think about it more than I think about Him. What I crave ends up ruling my life like a god. Anything I place above the true God in my priorities will eventually consume me and lead to trouble.

God made me (and you) for better things. The natural vacuum in each heart was meant to be filled with a relationship. We try to fill that void with all the things life has to offer, but that doesn't work because we were not created to find satisfaction in worldly "stuff." Colossians 3:1 & 2 says, *"Set your minds on things above."* Only a relationship with God can fill the empty places within a heart.

Bear by Carissa S.

When we seek God to satisfy our longings,
our appetites are likely to change
and we may find that things of this world
no longer seem so important.

DON'T LET THE WRAPPER FOOL YOU

Grocery shopping is hard work. With so many artificial additives in food, you have to scrutinize the gobbledegook on labels to be sure of what you're getting.

Have you ever bought something you thought was meat and then discovered upon closer inspection that it wasn't meat at all? What in the world is a by-product, anyway? According to Webster's Dictionary, by-product means an outgrowth, offshoot, or consequence of something else. What is an "outgrowth" or "consequence" of meat, and should we be eating it?

It's important to read labels on the backs of packages because what's on the front is often misleading. Unsuspecting parents buy so-called fruit snacks for their kids, thinking they are a nutritious alternative to junk food. In reality, they are 99 percent sugar with imitation fruit flavor and a bunch of chemicals thrown in, which I can't even pronounce. Why not just give your kid a banana? Advertising for juice drinks is just as misleading. Mostly water and sugar, they aren't even close to being real juice from a real fruit.

The problem of confusing labels and deceiving wrappers extends beyond the grocery store. In life, as well as on the pantry shelf, things wrapped in pretty packages often contain stuff that's not good for us and may even be dangerous. Likewise, what is good for our character sometimes doesn't look appealing at first glance.

For instance, God has wonderful gifts planned for us; but they often come "wrapped" in bad situations. Do you want to be strong and resilient, able to persevere and emerge victorious? These traits come from suffering through trials. Want to be patient? It's a result of waiting and waiting and trusting while you wait some more. We live in a world that focuses on instant gratification, so we are often so focused on the outside wrapping that we miss out on the gift inside.

Your desire is to be happy, but God's desire is for you to be holy. Yes, He wants to bless you, but the blessings He has in mind are things like strength and endurance. We often whine when these gifts come our way because we don't like the way they're wrapped.

When things seem hopeless to me and I can't imagine why God would allow a bad situation, I think about the day Jesus died. Imagine how his mother felt, standing at the foot of the cross looking up at her dying son who had been tortured. She must have wondered how and why God would allow such a situation. Imagine how the disciples of Jesus felt when He was arrested and killed. They had hoped that He would become an earthly king. They must have been devastated and confused. Yet, we know that the death of Jesus was a wonderful thing because of what it meant for us. At the time that He was dying, though, it must have seemed like God had made a terrible mistake or didn't care what was happening.

Let's admit it. We don't know what God has mind. Things may look awful to us, but there may be a very good reason for them to be happening. It just hasn't become apparent yet.

Just as our children don't know what's best for them, we as God's children often don't understand what we need either. We're convinced that life should be easy and happy all the time, but our Father knows better.

Isaiah 30:18 says, *"The Lord longs to be gracious to you."* If you look for God's gifts, you'll find them. But don't be distracted by the outward appearance. Trust that God has a great gift for you inside that unattractive wrapper.

> God doesn't cause suffering,
> but He does allow it
> in order to accomplish His purpose
> and to reveal His glory.
> He allows our hearts to be broken
> so He can get inside them.
> He doesn't promise a pain-free life;
> but He does promise His presence,
> even when we can't feel it.

CHOOSE TO DANCE

One of my favorite Bible verses begins with three powerful words: *"Choose for yourselves."* (Joshua 24:15) You and I really have only one basic choice to make in life and that core choice determines all our actions. It's the choice between right and wrong.

Choices have consequences and consequences affect not just us but others in this world. When we choose between right and wrong, we're making a multitude of other choices at the same time. We're choosing which results we want in our lives— either happy blessings or not-so-happy consequences. A choice can result in a peaceful, contented life or a life of trouble and sorrow. Ultimately, the choice between right or wrong is a choice of either eternal life with God or eternal separation from Him.

At the ripe old age of 120, Moses realized he wouldn't be leading the people of Israel much longer, so he gathered them together and passed on some guidelines for living. Deuteronomy chapter 30 tell us that Moses reminded the people of how God had always provided for and guided them. He recalled many commands of God and urged the people to obey them.

Moses explained that choosing God brings fulfillment, blessings, and life; but choosing against God brings emptiness, pain, and death.

In verse 15, Moses concluded his instruction to the people with these words: *"I set before you today life and good, death and evil. I command you to love the Lord and walk in His ways . . . and the Lord will bless you . . ."* Then in verse 19, Moses summed it all up saying, *"Love the Lord and obey His voice. Cling to Him. He is your life. I have set before you today life and death, choose life!"* Verse 19 describes how God rejoices when people turn to Him wholeheartedly, choosing to obey Him willingly.

Who, if they had the option, wouldn't choose life over death? Yet, we unwittingly make choices every day that lead down the path to "deathly" consequences. How, then, does one "choose life?" I think it's by learning to dance.

Let me explain. Since my brain has turned to lemon custard, I often use acronyms to help me remember things. The first letter of each word in a group is abbreviated into a more easily remembered word. So the word dance reminds me of five points to recall in order to choose life over death.

The first letter of the word dance is "D," which stands for determine. To choose life, I must determine to know God better by reading the Bible.

"A" stands for allow. Allow God to have control. I must give up my own ideas and desires.

"N" stands for never. Never stop learning what God desires. There's always more to learn, so I keep seeking His will.

"C" stands for choose. Choose to follow His plan. I trust that He knows best and I let go of my own plans.

"E" stands for express. I express my love and gratitude for Him by doing what He asks of me.

To choose life, I need to "dance" according to God's guidelines. Like the people Moses led through the desert, I need frequent reminders. That's why it's important for me to read the Bible often and memorize as much as possible. The more I fill my mind with God's words, the more those words influence my thoughts, decisions, and actions.

We all have choices to make. I hope you'll choose what's right. Choose God over the world. Choose the Bible over Miss Cleo. Choose giving over hoarding. Choose forgiveness over bitterness. Choose truth, love, and light.

Jesus said, *"I am the Way, the Truth and the Life."* (John 14:6) Choose Jesus. Choose *life!*

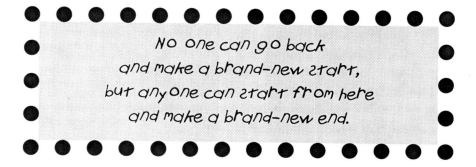

No one can go back
and make a brand-new start,
but anyone can start from here
and make a brand-new end.

MONSTER-IN-LAW

Jacob's father-in-law, Laban, wasn't a very nice guy. (Genesis 31) First, he made Jacob work seven years for permission to marry the girl he loved, Laban's daughter Rachel. Then, on the wedding day, the scoundrel deceived Jacob into marrying Rachel's sister Leah instead. (This girl must have been a dandy, if her dad had to trick somebody into marrying her.) Then Laban made Jacob work another seven years to win the woman of his dreams.

Even after Jacob became part of his family, Laban didn't give him any breaks. He made Jacob work six more years to obtain flocks of his own. Then the greedy cheat told Jacob, "The speckled and streaked ones will be your wages." He kept the best for himself and gave Jacob the rejects. Though Jacob worked diligently with all his strength, Laban continued to treat him unfairly, changing Jacob's wages ten times. He repeatedly made Jacob bear the losses while he kept the profits. This rat was determined to give his son-in-law a raw deal.

God, however, had other plans. And when God has a plan, nothing can thwart it. He was determined that Jacob would succeed, and Laban learned you can't keep God's man down.

God told Jacob, *"I have seen all that Laban has done to you."* Now, if I had been in Jacob's shoes, I might have answered, "You mean you've been watching all this and never jumped in to help me?" I probably would have questioned why God allowed this creep to succeed in his dastardly plans instead of zapping him with a lightening bolt. God, in His infinite wisdom, however, usually doesn't act the way I think He should.

If you're a parent to teenagers, you probably understand tough love. When teaching your kids a moral lesson, you don't protect them from uncomfortable situations. Instead, you allow them to endure difficulties long enough to sweat a little and learn from the experience. We all learn best from our mistakes, when there is nobody to bail us out. God allows us to endure situations rather than plucking us out of them, but that doesn't mean He deserts us. Like the trusty Mounties in silent movies, God shows up at just the right time.

Laban decreed that Jacob could only have the imperfect sheep, but God fixed him. He caused ALL the sheep born in Laban's herd to be spotted and streaked. Jacob's herd grew while his father-in-law's herd dwindled. Finally, Laban was getting what he deserved. If I were Jacob, I might have said "That's what you get you mean, old coot!" (As you can tell, God's not finished working on my attitude yet.)

The moral of this story is that control freaks like me shouldn't get flustered, frightened, or frustrated by calamities. Instead, we need to give up our unrealistic expectations, including the one that nothing bad should ever happen to us.

I'm working on burning this truth into my heart: Even when it doesn't look like it, God is in control and knows what I'm going through. He always has a plan in mind. And it will happen, in His time and in His way.

We usually can't see what possible reason God could have for allowing us to suffer; and we want to take matters into our own hands to correct the situation, but don't give up on God! No matter how unfairly you're treated or how heavily the odds weigh against you, if God wants something for you, it will work out.

Jacob didn't have to plot ways to outsmart his scheming father-in-law. He didn't need to take revenge. He kept doing the right thing and he waited for God to work. Just as God worked in Jacob's life, He can work in our lives too—so that His plan will be accomplished. Trust God, follow Him, then watch Him work.

God can transform trials into triumphs.

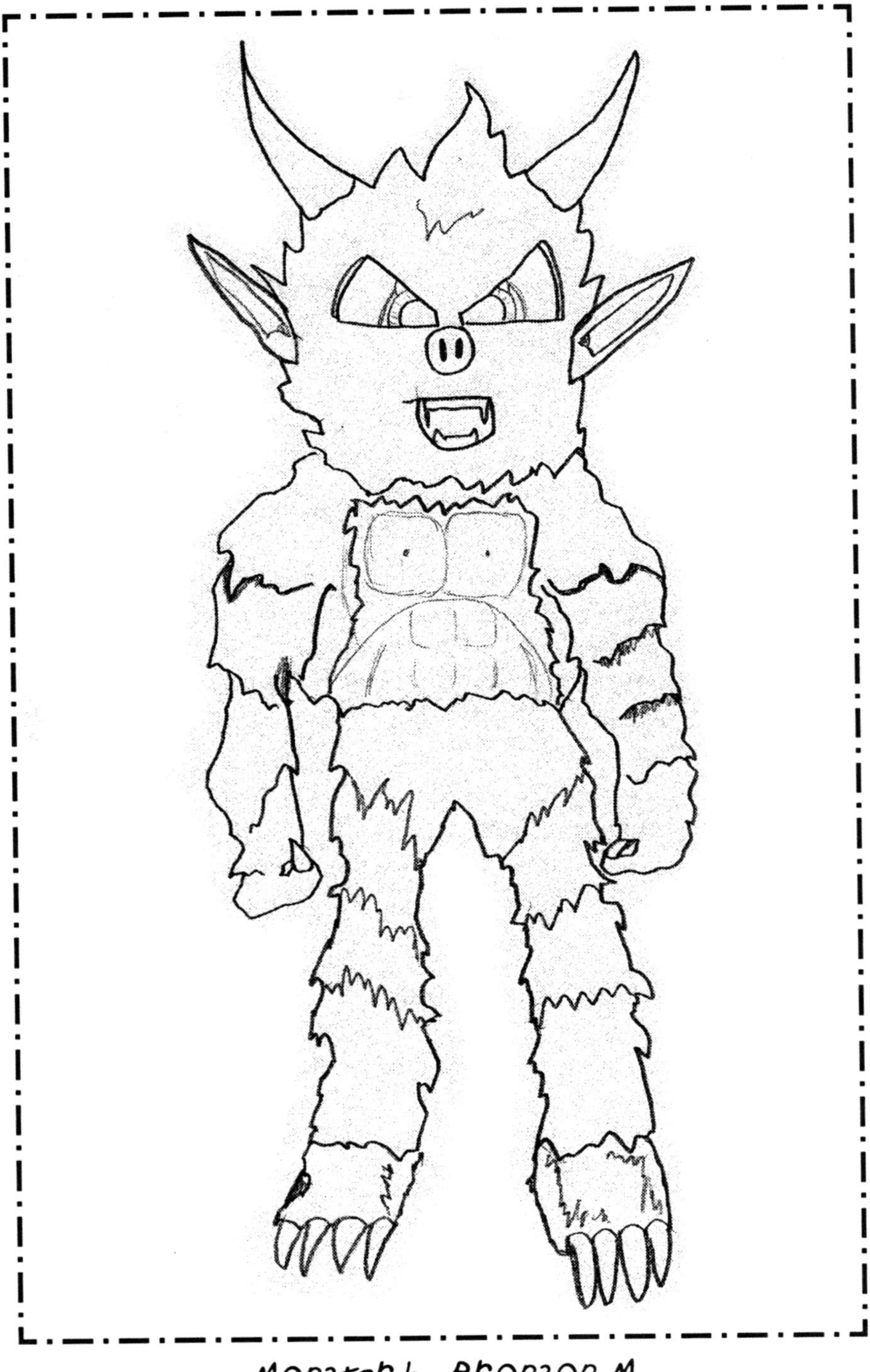

Monster by Bronson M.

MAKING GOD LAUGH

One snowy morning, I left church with a simple to-do list. It included: *Go to church, go home, and relax with the family.* Nowhere on the list was: *fishtail around an icy curve, become airborne, flip my van, barely miss a telephone pole, puncture the gas tank, and crash upside down in a cow pasture.* But that's just what I did.

My plans flew out the shattered windshield, as I peered out at the world upside down. (Does it turn your world upside down when things don't go as you'd planned?) Amid the odorous cow pies, I observed a herd of hefty Holsteins hot-footing it away from the accordion-shaped vehicle, which had sailed over the barbed wire fence.

This was not my idea of a fun afternoon. There I was, standing on my head, trying to pry open a door that was scrunched into the side of a hill. I smelled gas leaking into the van and I heard my knees knocking. As I pulled glass shards from my head, I envisioned this gas-filled time bomb exploding and blasting me heavenward like a circus clown from a canon. All I could do was tremble and pray. Once again, life had happened while I was making other plans.

While I did not fly to the moon, and my van did not explode, I was rescued by a passing motorist and whisked away in an ambulance to the Emergency Room. As is often the case, my plans changed in the blink of an eye.

When I think I've planned for all the details and I lay out the perfect blueprint for my life, here's what usually happens: The reality bird comes along and lays an ugly, giant egg in the middle of my agenda!

I've learned that, rather than falling into place, life will more likely fall to pieces. It's like an ice cream cone. I might think I have it licked; but then it drips all over me.

"But," I say to myself, "Life wasn't supposed to be this way!" I don't know about you, but I planned to stay healthy/wealthy/young/beautiful/married/happy/unwrinkled, stretch mark free, and flabless forever. (You can fill in your own blanks.)

Wait a minute. Am I looking at life from the viewpoint of what I want or from God's perspective of what is best?

Most people think God wants them to have an easy, comfortable life, getting what they want when they want it. While it's true that God enjoys giving good things to His children, they're often not physical things. He wants to provide invisible gifts, such as a closer relationship with Him.

God's ultimate goal is for me to become like Him. That doesn't happen when everything's rosy.

When my plans change, I tend to forget that God has a higher goal for me than just a life of ease. He wants to work on my heart and build my character. I believe God cares about my struggles and He hurts when I hurt, but what is most important to Him is developing in me faith, patience, goodness, and gentleness. In other words, God wants to make me like Jesus. Though He doesn't cause struggles and hardships, He uses them to accomplish His goals for my life.

According to Philippians 3:20, *"Our citizenship is in heaven."* We were created for a different life than this one on earth. This one is just a rehearsal designed to prepare us for the real thing.

When my plans don't succeed, I ask what God's plan might be. Could it be that He allowed a certain situation to redirect my focus? Could He be trying to get my tunnel vision off myself? Maybe He wants to lead me toward a closer relationship with Him.

Instead of telling God my plan and making Him laugh, maybe I should seek to know HIS plan and make Him smile.

HURTING OR HELPING?

Over and over, Cobi screamed, "No! No!" as the nurse and I held him down. He sobbed in pain and begged for my help, but all I could do was push him down onto the table with all my might as he kicked at me. The look of fear on his face burned a hole into my heart. As he struggled to get away, he kept his terror-filled eyes locked on mine as if to ask, "I thought I could trust you. Why are you hurting me?" I cried along with him, knowing that he depended upon me to protect him, but I could not free him.

Cobi, my grandson, was eighteen months old. He had third degree burns on his hand. Daily, the pediatrician had to "debride" the damaged tissue. That meant two people had to hold the screaming toddler down while the doctor ripped the skin from his hand so that it would heal properly. I would have given anything to trade places with Cobi, but I was helpless to stop his pain.

If you're a parent, you know how heart breaking it is to watch your children suffer. Yet, sometimes you must do just that, for their own good.

I can only imagine how painful debriding must be or how terrifying it is to be held down and subjected to such torture. But it was necessary for Cobi's healing. Without this treatment, he might have grown up without use of his hand, and his fingers may have permanently curled into his palm.

He didn't understand any of that, of course. All he knew was that strangers were hurting him and he couldn't get away. And someone he loved and trusted was helping these strangers to hurt him. He thought we were being cruel. It broke my heart to watch his suffering. Holding him down for it was the toughest thing I've ever done, but I had to do it. I know he was wondering, "If you love me, why won't you help me?"

Don't we ask the same question when God doesn't step in and rescue us from pain? Have you wondered, "Why is God punishing me? Why does He refuse to help me?" It's natural to ask, "Why?" But God's not going to send a telegram explaining His motives.

God is a loving parent who wants what's best for us. He cares about what we need, rather than what we want. He demonstrated how much He cares by sacrificing His son for us. Since He was willing to do that, I trust Him to do what's best for me in any situation.

Just as we parents must sometimes practice tough love with our kids, God is the same way with His children.

Even if I don't understand what He's doing or why, I can trust God. He's proven to be worthy of my trust. He has information that's not revealed to me. I can't figure it out, but I can focus on God's words.

We're like the passengers in the middle car of a long train. God is the engineer who sees the train from beginning to end and knows where it's going. Only He can look ahead to see how current problems may benefit us in the long run.

God allows challenges for reasons I will probably never understand. I do know it's not because He enjoys seeing me suffer. He may want to teach me to depend upon Him more, He may want to stretch my faith, or He might just want to wake me up.

He may allow suffering to soften and open my heart. He wants me to be still and listen to Him. Hardships remind me that I can't control everything.

No matter how abandoned I feel, I need to cling to the promise Jesus made when he said, *"I will never leave you nor forsake you."* (Hebrews 13:4-6)

Romans 8:28 says, *"We know that in all things God works for the good of those who love Him, who have been called according to His purpose."* This doesn't say that only good things will happen. It says that God can somehow bring something good out of even the worst situations, for those who love and serve Him.

When I see bad things happening and I can't understand why, I cling to my heavenly Father. It doesn't surprise me that I don't understand everything about Him or His word. Why shouldn't He write something more grand than what I can understand with my pinto bean brain?

When life doesn't go the way I plan, I take one day—and sometimes one moment—at a time, trusting God's wisdom. I rely on Him to carry me through.

I think that's the kind of trust and surrender He wants from all of us.

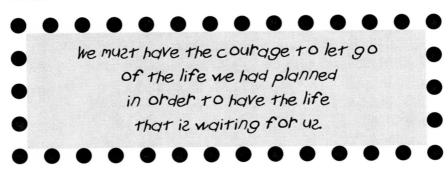

We must have the courage to let go
of the life we had planned
in order to have the life
that is waiting for us.

LIFE IN THE MANURE PILE

The husband once aspired to be a self-sufficient, back-to-the-land pioneer. He bought a windmill, oil lamps, beehives, and a couple of pigs, which we named Lois Lane and Clark Kent.

This dirty duo caused me headaches from the day we took them home. We tied them in gunny sacks and secured them in the back of our truck; but the Houdini hoglets somehow freed themselves, tumbled from the vehicle, and headed for the hills. We eventually got the slippery little buggers safely home, but only after a wild skirmish in the woods.

The adventurous and clever Clark soon discovered his alternate identity as Super Pig. He learned to climb atop his roofed shelter and leap over the fence to freedom. Lois, not to be outdone, was never far behind. Motorists on the highway near our home reported seeing wild pigs darting between cars. I also received some angry phone calls from horrified neighbors who were shocked to find the pair digging up their flower beds. Perhaps, rather than Lois and Clark, they should have been named Lewis and Clark, due to their propensity to explore.

These two heavy weights usually embarked upon their adventures while the husband was at work, so I was the designated pig herder, responsible for bringing the troops home after each rendezvous. How does one lure two full-grown hogs to follow you? It takes courage, determination, and a slop bucket full of swine delicacies like apple cores, potato peels, and moldy bread crusts. More than once, I trudged through waist-deep snow, dropping a trail of left overs behind me.

I've never liked animals that were too big to sit in my lap, but these humongous hogs were more than intimidating. They were man eaters! While leading them home like the pied piper, I had to run to stay one step ahead as they followed close behind, nipping at my heels.

Yes, pigs *bite*—at least these two did. They were scarier than attack dogs.

Once Lois and Clark tasted blood, they preferred it to their usual diet. That diet consisted of truckloads of stale doughnuts, sour milk, and assorted restaurant scraps. Keeping the porkers fed was a big job. They ate a lot, and you can imagine what else they did—a lot!

The manure pile grew into a mountain, which remained long after Lois and Clark were laid to rest as pork chops in our freezer.

The following summer, I planted a garden that I faithfully weeded, fertilized, and watered.

At the end of the season, I was shocked to discover that my prized vegetables were dwarfed in comparison to the giant tomatoes and cucumbers that had sprung up from the manure pile.

You may wonder why I'm telling you more than you care to know about pigs and manure. It's because I've found that where there's manure, there's sometimes a lesson buried under it.

Like you, I've known sorrow, loneliness, and disappointment. At those times, it often feels like I'm living smack dab in the middle of a mountain of manure. However, things that stink aren't necessarily bad. Sometimes, what we think is awful right now may end up being good for us. Ask anyone who took castor oil as a kid!

Just as the garbage in a compost heap makes gardens grow, the garbage in our lives can enhance our personal growth. Trials can result in strong faith and character. The stuff that stinks the most is usually the best fertilizer for healthy spiritual development. Even stinky manure, after a time, turns into healthy and clean smelling soil.

Gardens go through seasons. Spring is the season to plant and fertilize. Summer is the season to weed and cultivate. Fall is the season to harvest. Winter is the season for the land to rest. Our lives have different seasons too. Some of them are more difficult than others. But if we endure "for a season" without giving in to short-term thinking, we will reap a harvest.

When your heart is broken, it may feel hopeless; but there's always hope, even in the dung heap. Open your eyes to see beyond the pig pies to how God might be working. Consider what the end result, and God's plan, might be for this situation.

God can produce blossoms of blessing from pig manure. Well, the Bible doesn't actually say pig manure, but He can bring good from anything. Isaiah 61:3 says He will bestow upon those who grieve a crown of beauty instead of ashes, the oil of gladness instead of mourning, and a garment of praise instead of a spirit of despair.

God takes the smelly, disgusting manure that our lives can become and He brings forth prize-winning, life-giving fruit. Celebrate the fact that we don't have to climb that manure mountain alone. Believe and keep the faith, then grab a shovel and start digging. There's a harvest on the other side.

Pig by Shantel S.

Marsha Jordan

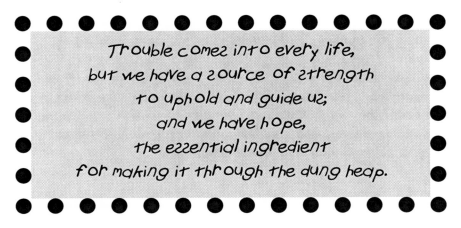

Trouble comes into every life,
but we have a source of strength
to uphold and guide us;
and we have hope,
the essential ingredient
for making it through the dung heap.

POOPED

Yesterday was one of those days. I was so pooped that I struggled to sit upright at the dining room table. It took extreme effort to hold my head up out of the soup bowl. Days like that are common for me because I have a connective tissue disease that causes chronic fatigue as well as pain.

If you've never experienced fatigue, you can't understand how debilitating it is. It's not the exhilarating tired you feel after aerobic exercising. It's not the contented tired you feel after gardening all day. It's more of a crash and burn, hit-the-wall, feel like you're dead or dying exhaustion. I think it must be the way the coyote feels after chasing the roadrunner all day and being pulled through a wringer, hurled off a cliff, blown up with dynamite, run over by a truck, squeezed through a knothole, and then having an Acme safe dropped on his head.

Exhaustion is the burn out toddlers experience after skipping their afternoon nap. I can relate when I see a two year old in a shopping mall throw himself to the floor sobbing. There are many days I feel like doing that, but I lack the energy required to cry.

The worst thing about chronic fatigue is that even after a full night's sleep, I still don't feel refreshed. Most mornings I wake up just as tired as I was when I went to bed. Fatigue is like a thirst that is never quenched or a hunger that's not satisfied. I rarely get "enough" rest.

Though I've dealt with weakness and fatigue for years, it still frustrates me. I get angry when the most strenuous activity I can accomplish is taking a shower. And I hate disappointing others by canceling outings because I need a hoist to lift myself off the couch. It's infuriating that I can be energetic and ambitious one day while the next day every cell in my body hurts and I need toothpicks to hold my eyes open.

Thinking about this recently got me so upset it triggered a hot flash. I decided to do something about it. So I started whining.

I've developed complaining to a fine art, but I've learned that it doesn't help the situation. In fact, focusing on the negative usually makes things seem even more miserable.

There's a passage in the Bible about weariness. Isaiah 40:29 says God gives strength to the weary and increases the power of the weak. It says those who hope in the Lord will renew their strength, run without growing weary, and soar on wings like eagles. Hmmm. I don't feel strong or powerful. I certainly don't soar, and I can't even remember when I ran last. Some days it takes all the energy I can muster just to move from lying to a sitting position. So what gives? Where's all this power that the Bible promises?

Obviously, God's not promising literal physical strength. In His perfect will, He knows that what we really need is inner strength.

And guess what. The best way to develop strength within is to face problems without. Problems like physical ailments and fatigue. Shucks! You didn't want to hear that, did you? Problems may wear down the body, but they can build up the spiritual "struggle muscles." When God gives strength to the weary, it may be in the form of perseverance, patience, determination, or greater faith. You may not run faster, jump higher, or leap Misery Mountain in a single bound; but you can likely feel your hope and your relationship with Him grow stronger.

God provides strength to battle discouragement, strength to remain obedient, strength to keep hope alive, and strength to endure.

The apostle Paul wrote to the Christians in Corinth about how he was physically persecuted, hard pressed, perplexed, and struck down, yet he did not despair. (2 Corinthians 4)

In the same way, even though my body isn't satisfied or renewed by physical rest, my soul can be satisfied by God. He revives my weary spirit with spiritual strength.

In 2 Corinthians, chapter 11, Paul listed some of his hardships, which included being beaten with rods, shipwrecked, stoned, imprisoned, flogged, and deprived of food, water, and sleep. He'd been naked, cold, and afflicted with a thorn in his flesh. Even so, he could say he delighted in his weakness, hardships, and difficulties. What was that? Delighted?! That must be a typo. He couldn't have said he was delighted, could he? Yes, that's what he said alright. Then he went on to say, *"God's grace is sufficient and His power is made perfect in weakness. When I am weak, then I am strong."*

Now when I consider the attitude Paul had, even in desperate situations, I (try to) replace my whining "Why me" attitude with a more submissive "Whatever you want for me, Lord." With a new perspective, I can hope for the best; but I also prepare for the worst. And then I accept whatever God sends.

Though I am weak and tired, I can be strong in His power.

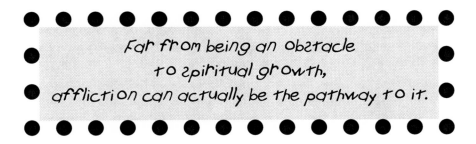

Far from being an obstacle to spiritual growth, affliction can actually be the pathway to it.

Weak and Strong by Shantel S.

WHO IS YOUR HERO?

Is your hero an athlete who kicks, hits, or throws a ball well? Or an actor who is envied for his good looks and great talent? Maybe it's a successful business person who invested well and grew rich.

My heroes are not actors, athletes, or millionaires. They are ordinary people like the veterans who defended our nation in times of war. They are small town folks who rally to help their neighbors.

Some of my heroes are fragile, gray-haired grandmothers who spend many hours at a computer keyboard sending encouragement and love to sick children via email. And some of my favorite heroes are gentle, loving mothers in cancer wards who rock their dying children as they cling to hope and pray for miracles.

Many of our nation's greatest heroes emerged from the smoking ashes of the World Trade Center towers on September 11, 2001. And many heroes never did emerge from that smoldering rubble.

One of my most beloved heroes is my dad. He's the most generous, honest, thoughtful, kind, and compassionate person I know. And he's cute, too. That runs in our family.

What makes a person a hero? Not super-human strength or uncommon abilities. Heroes are regular people who express extraordinary, self-sacrificing love. They give everything they've got for others.

I'm proud of the many unselfish American heroes our country has brought forth. Yet, they are only human, and they are not always able to save.

On my kitchen wall hangs a plaque with the words of President George Bush: "We will not tire. We will not falter. We will not fail." It's an admirable sentiment; but, sadly, human heroes do tire. Imperfect people have frailties and limitations. Sometimes they falter. Many times, in spite of great effort and the best intentions, they fail us.

There is only one hero who can never fail. He can always rescue. He, has the ultimate self-sacrificing love. His name is Jesus. He gave all that He could give in order to save those He loved – YOU and ME!

He is the greatest hero of all time.

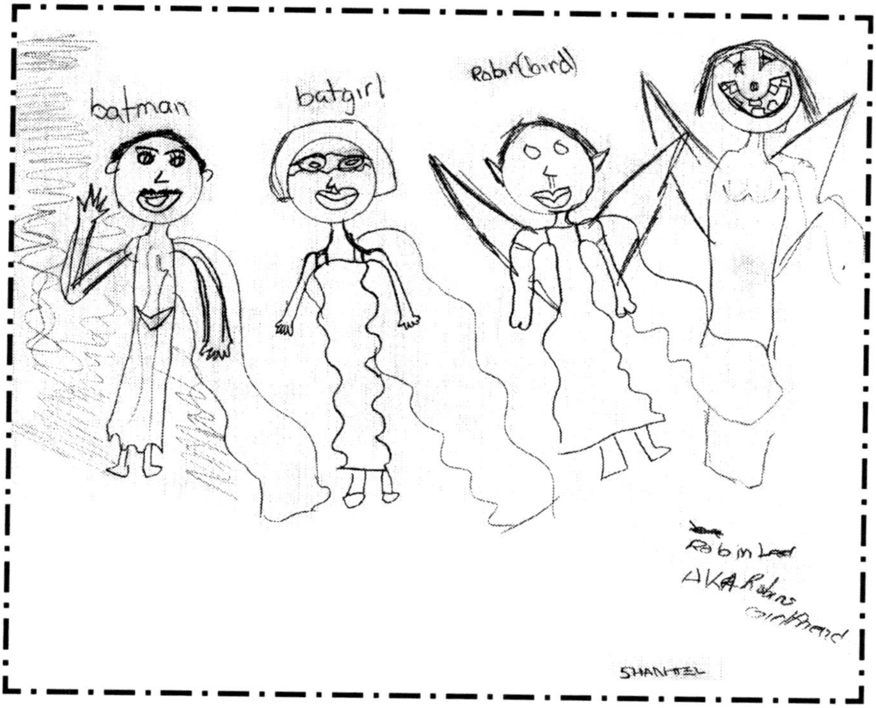
batman
batgirl
Robin(bird)
Robin
AKA Robins Girlfriend
SHANTEL

Heroez by Shantel S.

CHAPTER FOUR

CLINGING TO HOPE

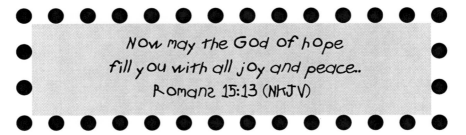

Now may the God of hope
fill you with all joy and peace.
Romans 15:13 (NKJV)

IT AIN'T EASY BEING BRAVE

A zoo attendant entered a lion cage carrying only a broom. He casually swept with no concern for the wild animal. He even poked the big cat with his broom. The lion hissed at him and moved to another corner of the enclosure. An onlooker remarked "You certainly are brave." The sweeping man chuckled and said, "I ain't brave, that old cat ain't got no teeth." In situations where there's not much danger, bravery comes easily. However, most of us face some very scary stuff. Having a sick child or losing your home, your income, your health, or your spouse can be terrifying. In circumstances like these, we can feel alone and vulnerable.

Children who feel that way curl up with a soft blanket or a cuddly teddy bear and feel more secure. But what can adults with big problems cling to? We need more than a piece of cloth or a toy to calm our fears.

When I'm scared, there are two sayings I like to remember: "To be afraid is to believe in evil more than you believe in God," and "Courage is fear that has said its prayers." Many people think being brave means having no fear, but courage is actually continuing on, *in spite of* fear. Those who believe that God is ultimately in control can trust Him to do the worrying.

When facing fear, if we don't turn to God, we're missing out. He can provide the courage we need. *"Be of good courage, and He shall strengthen your heart, all you who hope in the Lord."* (Psalm 31:24).

I taught my grandson this Bible verse: *"When I am afraid, I will trust in thee."* (Psalm 56:3) We sing it at bedtime to calm his fear of closet monsters, but this simple verse applies to my adult-sized fears as well. When anxiety descends like a heavy fog, these nine words can release fear's choke hold.

When the lions in life bare their teeth, I tell God my worries. Then I put my hope in Him. Remembering that He's with me calms my anxious thoughts. Revelation 5:5 says Jesus is the Lion from the tribe of Judah. A lion may be the king of the jungle, but Jesus is the king of kings. (Revelation 19:16) He is strong and mighty. He is never afraid. He is greater than the lions.

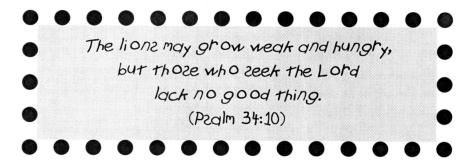

The lions may grow weak and hungry, but those who seek the Lord lack no good thing.
(Psalm 34:10)

WHAT IS GOD THINKING?

What can you say to a parent who loses a child to cancer? Whatever words we offer are inadequate to lessen their sorrow. We have no answers to questions like, "Why this child?" or "Why now?" and "What do I do now?"

Another question we all ask and cannot answer is, "Where was God and what was He thinking when this horrible thing happened?" For answers, I look to God's written word. It gives me a glimpse into His personality and thoughts.

If God were to telephone and speak to you during times of suffering, perhaps these are some things He might say:

"*I know how you feel.*" God understands the loss of a child because He experienced it. He said to Jesus, "*You are my son whom I love.*" (Mark 1:11) He watched men torture his beloved son. He felt the grief of seeing the people He'd created rebel against Him. "*His spirit was grieved.*" (Isaiah 63:10) The Bible says Jesus was "*a man of sorrows and familiar with suffering . . . He carried our sorrows.*" (Isaiah 53:3) Crucifixion was the most barbaric form of death known to man. It was a cruel, drawn out process. Nails were driven into wrists and ankles. The body was suspended in an abnormal position that crushed the lungs and heart. The pain was excruciating. For this torture, Jesus left the glory of heaven. He left the companionship of angels and the fellowship of His Father for this brutal treatment. He understands suffering like no other can.

In the midst of your struggles, God would say, "*I love you. I have loved you with an everlasting love.*" (Jeremiah 31:3) He demonstrated His great love with the ultimate sacrifice. "*God so loved the world that He gave His one and only son.*" (John 3:16)

He would say, "*You're not alone. I am with you.*" Deuteronomy 31:6 tells us, "*The Lord your God goes with you. He will never leave you nor forsake you.*" Isaiah 43:2 reads, "*When you pass through the waters, I will be with you.*" And Jesus said in Matthew 28:20, "*I am with you always.*"

He would say, "*I want to bless you.*" "*He did not spare his own Son, but gave him up for us all. Will He not also graciously give us all things?*" (Romans 8:32) Anyone who would give so great a gift at such a great cost must certainly have only our best interest at heart.

God would assure you that, "*Nothing bad in this world can separate us.*" "*Neither death, nor life, nor angels, nor demons . . . nor anything else in all creation can separate us from the love of God.*" (Romans 8:35-39)

God would tell you, "*Pain is part of life.*" "*In this world, you will have trouble.*" (John 16:33a)

But He would also say, "*Take heart.*" The next part of that verse says, "*But be of good cheer, for I have overcome the world.*"

He would tell you, "*Lean on me.*" "*Come to me you who are weary and heavy laden and I will give you rest.*" (Matthew 11:28)

He would say, "*Trust me.*" "*My peace I give to you . . . Do not be troubled and do not be afraid.*" (John 14:28)

He would promise, "*I can make you strong.*" "*My strength is made perfect in (your) weakness.*" (2 Corinthians 12:9)

He would say, "*I can bring good, even from tragedy.*" "*In all things, God works for the good of those who love Him.*" (Romans 8:28)

He would say, "*Ultimately, nothing—not even death—can hurt you, if you belong to me; because, through my son, you have the hope of eternal life.*" "*Death where is your victory . . . Where is your sting? Death has been swallowed up in victory.*" (1 Corinthians 15:55)

Even with the King of Kings leading us through life, it will be difficult; but we can endure, and even overcome, any struggle. He can strengthen us with the knowledge that no matter what happens in this lifetime, nothing here can steal our hope of the eternal treasure He wants to give us. He's created an everlasting kingdom where pain, suffering, tears and death will no longer exist; and He offers that home to all who will come.

Life may be filled with sorrow, but it won't be as hopeless with Jesus as it would be without Him.

When we're suffering, only God can provide the perfect peace for which our hearts long. God's love carries us through anything and overcomes any situation, burden, or grief—no matter how great.

The heart of Christianity revolves around a tragic and unjust death. The best man who ever lived—an innocent man—had to suffer, so how can we expect lives free from pain and sorrow? Yet, God brought life and good out of the tragedy of Jesus' death. He can do the same with our suffering too, if through that suffering we grow closer to Him.

Marsha Jordan

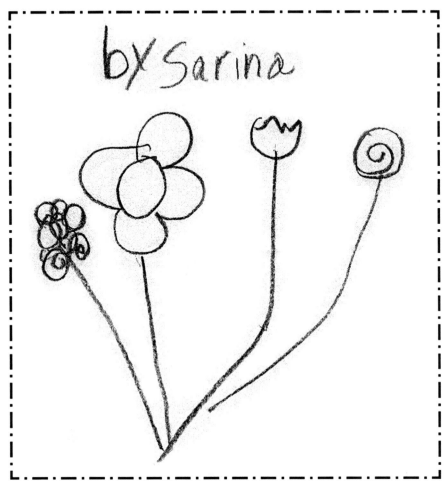

Flowers by Sarina S.

I believe in the sun even when it doesn't shine.
I believe in love even when it isn't shown.
I believe in God
even when I can't hear Him speak.
(written on the wall in a concentration camp)

DON'T BE SURPRISED

Life wasn't easy for cave men. They had to hunt all day, kill their dinner with a club, and drag the carcass to the cave. Then they had to butcher the animal and rub sticks together for a fire to cook it. They made clothes from the leftovers. And I think I have it rough when the husband wants me to cook instead of picking up carry out!

Life wasn't easy for our ancestors who crossed oceans seeking freedom. It wasn't easy for pioneers who fought wild Indians and settled the wilderness. Life has never been easy for past generations. It won't be any different for us.

I used to think I would arrive some day at that magical age when everything would be easy and problem free. Now I've wised up and learned this simple math equation: life = problems.

Trouble is a natural part of life like taxes, Big Macs, bad hair days, and *Leave it to Beaver* reruns. If you expect to have an idyllic life like Ward and June Cleaver, you may be in for disappointment. No matter how good life can be, there will always be some difficulty mixed in. Expecting to face some trouble can help us deal with it more effectively.

When Herbert Hoover decided to go into politics, he knew he would get criticism, but he went ahead anyway. Later he said, "When the criticism came, I wasn't surprised; I was better able to handle it."

The Bible confirms that hardships should not surprise us. The apostle Peter wrote, "Beloved, do not think it strange concerning the fiery trial, which is to try you, as though some strange thing happened to you." (1 Peter 5: 12, 13)

So why am I sometimes surprised when hassles come my way? Loved ones get sick or hurt, people lose jobs or homes. These things happen in life: car trouble, financial trouble, and in-law trouble. Unfortunately, none of us is exempt from problems. Do you sometimes feel that trouble attacks you like a swarm of angry bees? You swat one, and two more sneak up and sting you from behind. But don't let that depress you; we have hope!

I was shocked when I realized life isn't just about what I want, and I'm not here just to enjoy a pain-free life. When I asked myself what my life's purpose was, I realized God created me to get to know Him, to serve and glorify Him, and to become more like Him. The Bible says we need to be transformed. (Romans 12:2) That's not a miraculous happening. It's a process that involves problems. Problems are not only a normal part of life, but they're a necessary part too. They prepare us for the future. Not just the future five years from now, but also for the future that comes after our earthly lives end.

Only in heaven is life perfect and easy. But with each problem comes a chance to fulfill your purpose on earth, to learn something new, and to develop a more godly character. It can be difficult to remember this, though, when you're buried in heartache.

The good thing about pain is that it helps me put my focus where it should be, on the only one who can help me cope. When I practice depending upon Him rather than myself, I fulfill my purpose.

People often learn lessons during tough times that they could never have learned if life had been easy. I've found that I more fully enjoy beauty, since I nearly lost my ability to see it.

Think about a frightening circumstance you were forced to endure, and ask yourself what positive result came from it. Chances are you gained some special gift or grew spiritually in some way, not in spite of your ordeal, but because of it. That's why I say this life is merely a practice run or testing ground. It teaches us, stretches and sharpens us, strengthens us, and prepares us for eternity.

There are many unhappy endings in this life, but we can embrace hope knowing that the next life will not only be happier, but it will have no end.

When we understand that difficulties are inevitable and that we can't handle them on our own, we realize why it's important to develop a relationship with the all-powerful God before those trials come. It's good to know that we have a close relationship with, and are dearly loved by, the only one who can provide the strength, perseverance, and courage we will undoubtedly need throughout life. He's just waiting for us to ask for His help. *"He will surely be gra-*

cious to you at the sound of your cry; when He hears it, He will answer you." (Isaiah 30:19)

Bird by Doug V.

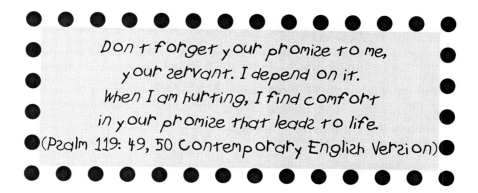

Don't forget your promise to me,
your servant. I depend on it.
When I am hurting, I find comfort
in your promise that leads to life.
(Psalm 119: 49, 50 Contemporary English Version)

WHY DOESN'T GOD ANSWER MY PRAYER?

I heard a story about a girl who wrote to a missionary. She'd been told not to request a response from him because missionaries are very busy. She wrote, "We are praying for you, but we are not expecting an answer."

Do you feel like God doesn't answer your prayers? Does it seem like He's not even listening? Actually, there is no such thing as an unanswered prayer. God does answer, but sometimes His answer is "No."

God is a loving parent, but His love means more than fulfilling our demands. He is not a parent who gives in to the whims of selfish children. He's not a bell hop who jumps at our command or a genie who provides everything we wish for. He's not a vending machine that spits out what we want when we push the right buttons.

Is it fair for us to run to God when we want something, but ignore Him and His laws the rest of the time? If we do not love Him, why do we expect Him to do as we command? That's like a child who rejects all his parents' teaching and doesn't care how much his lifestyle hurts mom and dad. Yet, when he wants something, he comes running to the parents that he doesn't even care about—just to use them when it suits him. Children often say things like, "If you love me, you'll give me what I want." That's not what love is about. Yet, we say this same thing to God, don't we?

God's ways are far above my ways, so I can't speak for Him. But I'm sure that it's just as difficult for Him to watch His children suffer as it is for us to stand by while our little ones are hurting. Sometimes even love must say, "No." Just as the pain of surgery is necessary to help a patient, emotional pain is sometimes necessary in our lives.

There is also the issue of free choice. Many of our grown children make deplorable choices. Sometimes, parents bail their kids out when they get into bad situations. But that sort of aid is often not helpful. It only enables children to continue in the destructive lifestyle. They know they will be rescued when the going gets tough. If they don't have to face the consequences of their behavior, why should they change? The same is true of all God's children. If He gave us everything we wanted, rewarding us for going against His wishes, what motivation would there be for us to live the way He wants us to?

Would we even care about His wishes or feelings?

It's also possible that what we interpret to be an answer of "no" from God may just be Him telling us to wait a while. He is the creator, we're the creation. He's the potter, we're the clay. (Isaiah 64:8) Can the clay tell the potter what to do or when to do it? (Isaiah 29:16 and 45:9)

There are three things I know for sure:

1) God loves me.

2) He has all knowledge, so He knows what's best.

3) He has all power and can do anything.

When I put those three things together (He can do anything, He loves me, and He knows what is best), then I am able to trust His decisions and His timing, whether they make sense to me or not.

Whether His answer to prayer is a "Yes," a "No," or a "Wait," I need to let God answer in His own time, in His own way.

God is near the broken hearted.

LIFE'S TEST

(Written by Susan Richard, used by permission)

In my life, I've searched high and low.
I've searched my heart, my mind, and soul.
I've searched the secrets of my past.
I've revisited all the why's I'd asked.
I've knelt down on my knees and prayed.
Sometimes for hours, that's where I've stayed.
I've cried and wept, sometimes nonstop.

Marsha Jordan

But God, He bottles every drop.
He never leaves my side, I know.
He allows some pain to help me grow.
These trials of life will one day pass,
And then there'll be no why's to ask.
So I'll just smile and thank the Lord
For all the promises in His word.
I'll trust, confessing He knows best.
And then He'll say, "You've passed life's test!"

I passed the test! by Cobi J.

Through hardships, God is training me,
so should I try to avoid them?
Rather than disasters turning people into
critics of God,
they should turn them into pursuers of God.

WHAT DID I DO TO DESERVE THIS?

"You must have done something awful for this to happen to you." Has anyone ever said that to you? Have you said it to yourself? Job had been through a lot. He'd lost his children, his home, his possessions, and his health. All he had left was his wife, and that was not necessarily a good thing. She wasn't much help to him during his troubles. Job needed some encouragement. He needed to know somebody cared and sympathized with him. He needed friends.

His friends came to see him, alright. But they didn't provide what he needed. Instead, they told Job that he must have committed some horrible sins and that God was punishing him by sending all these calamities.

Many people think this way. They believe anything bad that happens must be punishment from God. Let's see what God has to say about that.

In Job 1:8, God said there was nobody else on earth like Job. He was *"blameless and upright. He feared God and shunned evil."* So why did so much evil befall Job? Because the devil complained to God that the only reason Job was so good was because God had given him so much. Satan thought if everything was taken away from Job, then he would not be loyal to God.

God knew how Job would react, though, and He wanted to show other people and Satan the sort of example Job was going to set. Even when Job's wife suggested that he curse God and die, Job refused to denounce God or blame him.

God often uses people in difficult circumstances to teach others. (John 9:1-3) Jesus deliberately delayed going to see Lazarus when He'd been told his friend was sick. After Lazarus died, Jesus brought him back to life. Do you think that Jesus planned it that way, so that people could see His power? By allowing Lazarus to die, Jesus was able to teach others and to make it clear to them that He was the Son of God (John 11:15, 42).

There are many examples in the Bible of righteous people suffering through no fault of their own. Abel was killed by his evil brother who was jealous. Joseph was put into prison because of a wicked and deceitful woman, not because he'd done anything wrong. John the Baptist was beheaded, though he was a prophet of God. Jesus said there was no other man like John, but he died because of a woman who sought revenge.

Here's what Peter wrote to New Testament Christians about suffering: "You greatly rejoice, though now for a little while you may have had to suffer grief in all kinds of trials. These have come so that your faith—of greater worth than gold, which perishes even though refined by fire—may be proved genuine and may result in praise, glory and honor when Jesus Christ is revealed." (1 Peter 1:6-7)

Suffering is greater than gold, which doesn't last, because suffering refines our faith and makes it genuine. This results in honor for Jesus.

And, speaking of Jesus. He was innocent, yet he suffered more than anyone. He willingly left heaven to suffer cruelties he didn't deserve and he didn't have to accept. It's hard enough to endure trials when we can't do anything to stop them. Think of how tempting it would be, if you had the power to call angels to help you or if you could strike dead anyone who tried to harm you? Jesus had the power to avoid suffering, yet he gave up His right to do that and instead faced the pain . . . for us.

We may suffer a lot of pain in our lives, *but* when this life is over, we do not need to suffer through eternity. Why? Because of the suffering Jesus took on himself for us. He suffered because He didn't want us to suffer. Does that sound like a God who is waiting for an opportunity to punish us when we do wrong? Jesus came to this world to seek and save. He was led like a lamb to the slaughter, and it was because He wanted to spare us from eternal suffering.

So the next time trouble comes into your life, please don't blame God for it. He's not sitting on His throne looking for a reason to zap you. He made the supreme sacrifice in order to SPARE us from suffering the punishment we deserved for our sins.

Will you allow your pain to turn you away from the one who wants to rescue you from it? That's what Satan would like to see. May we, like Job and Peter, allow our suffering to refine our faith and result in God's praise, glory, and honor.

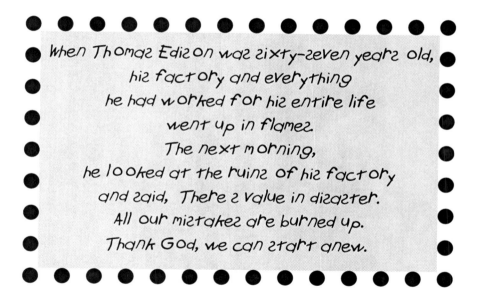

When Thomas Edison was sixty-seven years old,
his factory and everything
he had worked for his entire life
went up in flames.
The next morning,
he looked at the ruins of his factory
and said, There's value in disaster.
All our mistakes are burned up.
Thank God, we can start anew.

A summer day by Tiara B.

MORE THAN YOU CAN HANDLE?

There's a dangerous illness afflicting women everywhere across the nation. It's linked to considerable physical and mental suffering. It disrupts millions of lives, decreasing productivity and contributing to marital stress, absenteeism, loss of income, and disability. It is depression.

118

Depression may not be as obvious as a broken leg, but it's just as real and just as painful. It's a complicated "whole body" illness that affects the way you eat, sleep, think, behave, and feel. It's a very treatable condition, so there is no need to suffer with it. Unfortunately, within the Christian community, there are four common misconceptions about this illness, which make it difficult for many to seek the help they need. These myths are:

1) God doesn't give us more hardship than we can handle.
2) Good Christians don't get depressed.
3) Depression is sin.
4) We're useless when we're depressed.

Many well meaning people tell the depressed person that God doesn't give you more than you can handle, so He must think you can bear whatever He has dumped in your lap. People who think this way claim that this idea is taught in 1 Corinthians 10:13. What this verse actually says is that you will not have any *temptation* that isn't common to men, and that God will not allow you to encounter any *temptation* to sin without also providing a way for you to avoid that *temptation*. In other words, God won't let you be tempted when there is no way you can resist sinning.

Does God allow his people to be burdened beyond what they're able to bear? Paul wrote these very words in his second letter to the Corinthian church. He said, *"We were under great pressure, far beyond our ability to endure , so that we despaired even of life."* (1 Corinthians 1:9) Paul's difficulties were too much for him. If God doesn't give more than a person can bear, He certainly would not have excessively overburdened the apostle Paul, would He?

Paul was suicidal and no longer wanted to live. That's about as depressed as you can get, so how can anyone say that Christians don't or shouldn't get depressed? Paul was a leader of the Christian church. If he got depressed, can we expect to be immune to depression? But don't despair about that, because Paul wrote, *"But He (God) delivered us and He will deliver us."* Even if the situation ends in death, God delivers His people. Paul wrote in 2 Timothy 4:16-22, *"The Lord stood at my side and gave me strength, so that through me the message might be fully proclaimed . . . and I was delivered from the lion's mouth. The Lord will rescue me . . . and will bring me safely to His heavenly kingdom."* God helps us through tough times IF we allow Him to handle things and give Him room to work. Paul said *"When I am weak, then I am strong."* (2 Corinthians 12:10)

Some of God's greatest leaders suffered from depression. There was the prophet Elijah. In 1 Kings 19:4, it says, *"He came to a broom tree, sat down under it and prayed that he might die. 'I have had enough, LORD,' he said,'Take my life.'"*

David, the "man after God's own heart," got depressed. The book of Psalms is filled with expressions of his depression. He wrote, *"I am laid low in the dust."* (Psalm 119:25) *"I am troubled, I am bowed down greatly; I go mourning all the day long. I groan because of the turmoil of my heart."*(Psalm 38:6,8-NKJV) In Psalm 6:3 he says, *"my soul is in anguish."* Verses 6 and 7 say, *"I am worn out from groaning; all night long I flood my bed with weeping and drench my couch with tears. My eyes grow weak with sorrow."* King Solomon wrote in Proverbs 18:14, *"The spirit of a man will sustain him in sickness, But who can bear a broken spirit?"* Others in the Bible who may have experienced depression include Job, Jonah, and Jeremiah (called "the weeping prophet").

Nowhere does the Bible call depression sin. 2 Corinthians 7:6 says God comforts the depressed; He doesn't condemn them. Depression is an illness. A person cannot talk themselves out of it any more than they can talk themselves out of Chicken Pox, Diabetes, or Cancer.

Rather than being useless when in the throes of depression, we can be very useful to God when we have more than we can handle. It's at those times when we are at the end of our own strength that God can work best through us. In 2 Corinthians 12:9, Paul wrote, *"He said to me, 'My grace is sufficient for you, for my power is made perfect in weakness.' Therefore I will boast all the more gladly about my weaknesses, so that Christ's power may rest on me."*

When God allows trials to come into our lives, Peter says it's *"so that your faith will be proved genuine and may result in praise, glory, and honor when Jesus Christ is revealed."* (1 Peter 1:6,7)

God's strength takes over and gets us through, when we've reached the point of more than we can handle on our own. (John 15:5 says, "*Apart from me you can do nothing.*") This is why Paul boasted about his weaknesses instead of trying to hide them. He acknowledged that he had no strength himself, yet he was more than a conqueror (Romans 8:37) by God's strength and power, which worked through him.

Depression can be a struggle, but it can also be a gift. The person who has experienced it can help others through it. Only one who knows first hand how it feels to despair of life can offer compassion and understanding to a fellow sufferer. This kind of empathy is not possible for someone who has never felt for themselves the hopelessness of depression.

"Not by might, nor by power,
but by my spirit, saith the Lord of hosts"
(Zechariah 4:6)

We can't conquer depression
by our own power.
We must rely on God for strength to do
what He wants us to do.

TEN TIPS FOR BEATING DEPRESSION

I heard about a woman who was suffering from depression, so her concerned husband took her to a psychiatrist. The doctor listened to the couple talk about their relationship, and then he said, "The treatment I prescribe is really quite simple." With that, he went over to the man's wife, gathered her up in his arms, and gave her a big kiss. He then stepped back and looked at the woman's glowing face and broad smile. Turning to the woman's husband, he said, "See! That's all she needs to put new life back into her." Expressionless, the husband said, "If you say so, Doc, I can bring her in on Tuesdays and Thursdays."

Okay, that's not how to treat depression, but I have a few other suggestions that make more sense. As a result of trial and error, over the course of thirty years, I've found ten blues battling strategies that often help me. These are not quick fixes, and this list is not exhaustive. It is also not a "must do" list.

When you're depressed, the last thing you need is a list of expectations to live up to. Don't stress about forcing yourself to accomplish all these things. They're not items to be checked off a list each day. The only one that is crucial is number one. After that, you can experiment with the others as you feel able to.

1) GET THE FACTS AND GET HELP.

Web sites and books on depression abound. Find them and do some research. You need to know what you're dealing with. Learn all you can about depression, so you can make educated decisions about your own health, learn how others cope, and find what medical treatment is available. Many books have self tests to help you determine whether you are experiencing clinical depression or temporary sadness in reaction to an event. In addition to reading everything you can get your hands on, one of the most important things you can do for yourself is seek medical help right away. Depression is much too complicated for you to solve on your own. Clinical depression is a serious medical condition that is very complicated to treat. Often it is a physical problem that requires long term medication. In my own experience, it's taken years of medication, counseling, and practicing various self help methods to slowly emerge from it, and it's still a daily battle.

Many people suffer needlessly from depression because they won't consult a doctor. If you're waiting for God to heal you, consider this: God gives scientists intelligence, which they often use to create helpful medicines; and He gives doctors wisdom to treat illnesses. Wise doctors and modern medicines are gifts from God and vehicles through which He often heals. Doctors can help you determine whether what you feel is truly depression, or if you are just reacting normally to a sad life situation.

If you've experienced depression, you already know it is not an illness you can "snap out of," no matter what others may tell you. It's not something to be ashamed of either. Depression can be a serious physical illness caused by an imbalance of brain chemicals or other factors. Like any serious medical condition, depression needs to be treated. Without the proper treatment, none of my suggested coping strategies will do any good.

2) GET FOCUSED.

Feelings of hopelessness and helplessness pervade the life of a depressed person. The opposite of depression is a hopeful attitude. Focusing on hope and developing a hopeful heart is a must. It can be accomplished in a couple ways. One way is to search the Bible for the numerous Scriptures that tell how God has helped those who felt hopeless. It's helpful to memorize verses like these: Hebrews 4:15 *"For we do not have a high priest who is unable to sympathize with our weaknesses, but we have one who has been tempted in every way, just as we are—yet was without sin."*; 2 Corinthians 4:8 & 9 *"All-surpassing power is from God and not from us. We are hard pressed on every side, but not crushed; perplexed, but not in despair; persecuted, but not abandoned; struck down, but not destroyed."*; Matthew 6:34 *"Therefore do not worry about tomorrow, for tomorrow will worry about itself. Each day has enough trouble of its own."*; Isaiah 41:10 *"Do not fear, for I am with you; do not be dismayed, for I am your God. I will strengthen you and help you; I will uphold you with my righteous right hand.";* and John 14:27 *"Peace I leave with you; my peace I give you. I do not give to you as the world gives. Do not let your hearts be troubled and do not be afraid."*

The story of Job and the book of Psalms are the most worn pages in my Bible. While at my lowest, I've read and re-read them more times than I can count. My fridge and the mirrors in my house are covered with sticky notes reminding me of how God intervenes in the lives of His people.

Another way to focus on hope is by practicing positive self talk. This simply means telling yourself good things. I made a list for myself of positive affirmations like "God cares and understands my pain. God values me. God is giving me strength. I am made in God's image. I can choose my attitude. I choose not to put myself down. I'm a worthwhile person. I have a purpose. I enjoy life. I choose to be happy and I am competent." If you struggle with depression, I think you'll find it helpful to write down as many of these affirmations as you can think of and read them every day. Even if they're not currently true or you don't really believe them, it's okay. Say them to yourself anyway. Your mind will come to believe what you tell it, so tell it you are already the type of person you want to become. Be sure to remind yourself often that God is with you and He is pouring his strength on you. *"Why are you cast down, O my soul? And why are you disquieted within me? Hope in God, for I shall yet praise Him For the help of His countenance. For You are the God of my strength."* (Psalm 42:5 and 43:2 NKJV)

2 Corinthians 4:18 says we need to *"fix our eyes not on what is seen, but on what is unseen. For what is seen is temporary, but what is unseen is eternal."* Focusing on positive, heavenly things rather than earthly things will keep the feelings of hopelessness at bay.

3) GET FRIENDLY.

Fellowship with other people is a mood lifter. Being alone is the worst thing you can do when you're depressed. Unfortunately, it's usually the very thing I want most. Depression grows best in isolation. I find it very difficult to get out and socialize when I'm depressed, but if I push myself to do it, I'm almost always glad later. Some ideas for socializing include joining a club, taking a class, inviting someone to meet you for lunch, or visiting a nursing home to chat with the residents there. It especially helps me to be with friends who enjoy the same hobbies I do. Shopping, watching movies, and rubber stamping are some of the things I enjoy doing alone, but they're twice as much fun when I do them with friends.

4) GET GIGGLING.

I collect cartoons and funny newspaper columns. I visit humor web sites online, watch funny movies, and read funny books. Best of all is laughing with friends. One of the reasons I enjoy my grand-son so much is because he makes me laugh. I can act goofy with him and let go of my inhibitions. We dance and sing and make up silly rhymes. I have photographs of us wearing funny glasses with big black mustaches. I laugh every time I look at those. Laughing affects brain chemicals. It releases endorphins, which make you feel good. Chocolate does the same thing, but a good laugh is less fattening.

A friend of mine, who had a very frustrating job, told me that one day she was inspired by someone who had a huge, bright smile. She decided to emulate that woman and smile at everyone she encountered. Right away, she realized that smiling was addictive. It seemed to make the time pass more quickly and she found herself less frustrated and more at peace. She told me, "It sounds corny, but it really works!" Paul wrote, "*Rejoice in the Lord always. Again I will say rejoice!*" (Philippians 4:4 NKJV) I've heard that a person can act her way into feeling better. Act happy, act glad, and it helps you to feel happy and glad. Paul exhibited this truth in his own life. Acts 16 tells how Paul and Silas were attacked, beaten, locked in stocks, and thrown into solitary confinement. Yet, at midnight, what were they doing? Feeling sorry for themselves? Asking God, "Why?" Moaning and complaining like I do? No, they were singing! Sure they were suffering, but they knew they were children of God. Paul may have even been remembering his personal encounter with Jesus on the road to Damascus. (Acts 22:10) They were praising God because they had been rescued from their sins, filled by the Holy Spirit, and added to God's family. No jailer could take that away. That was worth being grateful for, no matter what else happened to them. Even if they were to be killed, it would only send them to heaven. So why should they fear? That's some awesome faith, isn't it?

5) GET RHYTHM.

When I feel a case of the gloomies descending, that is not the time to play melancholy music. Positive upbeat tunes are in order—the sort of music you might hear at a parade or a circus. Music gets your toes tapping and your blood flowing. It makes you want to sing. Singing and dancing sends a message to your brain that you're happy. Your brain is an actualizer. Whatever it "thinks" is true, it works to bring about. This is why positive thinking works. You tell yourself, "I'm happy" often enough and your brain accepts it as fact. It actualizes that truth, making it happen. I've found that when depression takes hold of me, I tend to ruminate on negative thoughts. Listening to good, Christian music with positive lyrics helps to pour good things into my brain and crowd those negative things out. There's a list of good things to ponder in the fourth chapter of Paul's letter to the Philippian church. It says to think about whatever is true, honest, just, pure, lovely, noble, right, or admirable. Philippians 4:8 says, "If anything is excellent or praiseworthy, think about such things." Christian music helps me accomplish this.

6) GET BUSY.

We all need to feel like we're involved in something significant. We need to participate in something outside ourselves. You might consider volunteering at a local women's shelter or food pantry. I've enjoyed both and discovered that when I stay busy helping others and concentrating on their problems, I get a break from focusing on my own troubles. This is how Hugs and Hope began. It started with a small effort to make a difference for one family and it grew. I've learned that joy boomerangs. When you give it away, it comes back to you. Helping others gives you the heart-warming satisfaction of knowing you are making a difference in the world. That will elevate your mood as well as your self esteem.

7) GET PHYSICAL.

This is two-fold. Physical exercise is good for us, but physical contact is equally important. Our bodies need to move to be healthy, and going for a walk is the easiest exercise for me to do when I'm depressed. It doesn't require as much energy and motivation as other activities. Breathing the fresh air and looking at the beauty of nature can be helpful, and taking my dog along is even better. Just watching his ears flop as he bounces down the road in front of me often brings a smile to my face.

Exercise affects brain chemicals, and the healing touch of physical closeness does too. If you're depressed, hug somebody—anybody, everybody! A hug is good medicine. It reduces stress and tension and it boosts your immunity to illness. Hugs raise self esteem and lower blood pressure. They feel good and make people happy. And they're free! Hugs are the universal language that communicates love and acceptance. They're healthy for the "hugger" as well as the "hugee."

8) GET QUIET.

I need to lean heavily on God's word and spend time with Him. When I pray, I talk things over with God. When I read the Bible and meditate on it, I hear Him speak to me and I contemplate what He says. I've found this to be one of the best anti-depressants there is. However, I need to add a word of caution here. Too much solitude can worsen depression. Isolating yourself and avoiding people can make depression grow. Don't use meditation time as an excuse to avoid human contact. Time with God is of the utmost importance, but balance between quiet time alone and time spent with others is essential.

9) GET FORGIVENESS -- AND GIVE IT TOO!

I've read that many psychiatrists agree that depression is guilt or anger turned inward. David is an example of someone whose guilt led to depression. After committing adultery, he wrote, "*When I kept silent, my bones grew old through my groaning all the day long. For day and night Your hand was heavy upon me; My vitality was turned into the drought of summer.*" (Psalm 32:3-4)

Sin makes you feel bad, but when you receive God's forgiveness, your guilt is removed; and often depression is removed too.

Depression can sometimes be caused from the need to forgive someone else or yourself (whomever is making you angry). Grudges cause feelings of frustration, which aggravate the hopeless feelings of depression. When we forgive, we let go of past hurts and give up bitterness. Then depression has no negativity on which to feed. If you free yourself from feelings of hate and open yourself up to feelings of love, you may feel as if the depression is physically lifting off your shoulders.

My friend Nance went through a difficult divorce, which left her bitter about the past, anxious about the future, and miserable in general. She harbored a lot of grudges and guilt, and she worried constantly. She felt the need to control everything in her life, yet she knew she couldn't. After attending a women's retreat, Nance realized what her negativity was doing to her. She released her worries, fears, anger, and resentments at the foot of the cross. Then she felt a renewal in her heart. She was happy and at peace.

When she was dying, Nance told me that the most difficult thing she'd ever had to do was forgive—both her ex-husband and herself—for past mistakes. She said forgiving was even harder than dying!

Forgiveness isn't a simple one time event. It's a process that often takes time (sometimes years), but it's an important step to healing.

Jesus taught forgiveness when he said we'd be forgiven in the same way we forgive others, and when he told Peter we should forgive, not seven times, but seventy times seven. Of course, Jesus also *lived* forgiveness. While hanging on the cross, he looked at his torturers and said, *"Father forgive them for they do not know what they are doing."* (Luke 23:34)

10) GET THANKFUL.

When I'm depressed, I need to make a conscious effort to count my blessings. An attitude of hopelessness and discontent has a hard time competing with an attitude of gratitude. 1 Thessalonians 5:28 says, *"In everything give thanks, for this is the will of God in Christ Jesus for you."* It's important to remember that depression is not fatal and it doesn't last forever. You WILL survive! Remind yourself that this cloud of despair will pass eventually. It may seem like there's no light at the end of the tunnel, but trust that there is; and be thankful for that, as you wait for the light to appear.

So, while kisses from your husband (or a psychiatrist) may be great, they can't cure depression. But along with medication and the proper treatment, now you have some practical steps you can take for your own well being. There are times when one of these strategies may be more helpful than the rest. Other times, it may seem that none of them makes a huge difference. But I keep practicing all of them anyway, because I know they are steps toward a healthier lifestyle. Following them on a regular basis may not eliminate depression forever, but they help me to minimize the severity.

These tips can be helpful for people who are not depressed too. They can be useful for anyone who is a little discouraged or needs to refocus on more positive things in life.

I hope that by trying these ideas you may find yourself on the way to experiencing more joy.

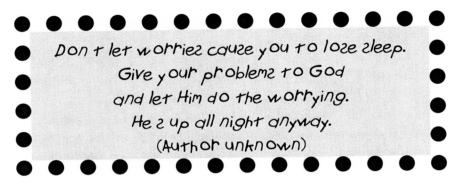

Don't let worries cause you to lose sleep.
Give your problems to God
and let Him do the worrying.
He's up all night anyway.
(Author unknown)

ONE WOMAN'S STORY

Sharon was talking to a friend on the phone one night. When her friend asked, "How are you?" Sharon suddenly exploded with emotion. Without warning, she began sobbing and literally collapsed in a heap on the floor. Her friend came over and took Sharon's kids for the night. Sharon cried for hours till she fell asleep. It was only the first of many sleepless nights.

She cried every day for months, never knowing when she might break down. She didn't need a reason. While driving to work in the morning, she would burst into tears. She worried about embarrassing herself, so she stayed home more and avoided people as much as she could.

Isolating herself made her feelings of loneliness worse. "Nobody understands what I'm going through," she told herself. She felt that her life was worthless because she could no longer function. She couldn't sleep, eat, or focus on anything. She was irritable and couldn't seem to get along with anyone anymore. She was disappointed and ashamed that she had let herself sink so low. She tried her best to pull herself out of this "funk." But she felt stuck. She felt guilty because her family deserved better treatment than she was able to give them. She concluded that they would be better off without her.

One day, while having an annual medical exam, Sharon's doctor asked how things were at home. Sharon began crying uncontrollably. When her doctor suggested that she was suffering from clinical depression, Sharon was surprised. She should have known, but she didn't.

The doctor prescribed anti-depressants and made an appointment for Sharon to talk with a therapist. Sharon didn't notice any improvement for a couple of weeks. It started slowly, but she gradually began to feel more peaceful and content. At this point, she was able to think more clearly and tackle small steps, one at a time, to work toward taking charge of her mental health. As Sharon took better care of herself, she grew stronger, which helped her to continue on the path to wellness.

When she met with her doctor for a six week follow up, she told him, "I just wish I had sought help earlier. I could have avoided so much pain."

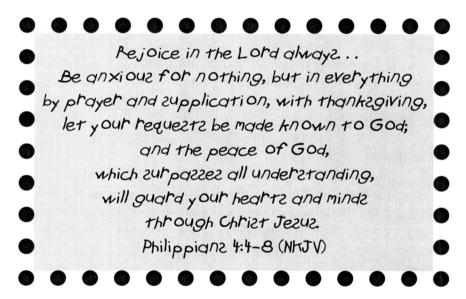

Rejoice in the Lord always...
Be anxious for nothing, but in everything
by prayer and supplication, with thanksgiving,
let your requests be made known to God;
and the peace of God,
which surpasses all understanding,
will guard your hearts and minds
through Christ Jesus.
Philippians 4:4-8 (NKJV)

WHY DOES GOD ALLOW SUFFERING?

Justin was a typical ten year old boy. He liked Legos, trains, and watching TV. He had red hair, freckles, and a huge smile. Justin was a great kid and everybody loved him. Because of cancer, he didn't live to see his eleventh birthday. His mom Mary, who had watched him suffer for months, held her son in her arms when he died.

Every day, for the last two years, she has lived with the grief of her loss and the memories of Justin's suffering.

This issue of suffering is the most common argument against religion. People often ask, "If there is a loving God, why does He make people suffer?"

I firmly believe that God does not cause sickness or pain. He doesn't make people hurt, and He doesn't want them to suffer. The life of Jesus proved this. He cured people; He did not make them sick. Why, then, are so many in pain?

There is no easy answer. To try and understand, I step back and look at the big picture. God made everything perfect. Then man sinned and that perfection was spoiled. Now we live in a world where evil abounds. We are subject to the evil actions of sinful people and to the natural consequences of those actions. This is not at all what God intended for the world He created.

God can and does intervene in some events, but why not others? Only He knows that answer, but the Bible teaches that there will be a time when He will put an end to ALL death, sadness, pain, sickness, and suffering.

Below are some possible reasons that people suffer.

1) We do things ourselves that cause us pain. We don't eat right, so we have heart attacks. We drive fast, so we have accidents. We smoke, so we get cancer. We start wars, we break laws, we don't show love to our fellow man. Much of the sorrow in this world, we bring upon ourselves by our own actions.

2) But what about innocent children who are not responsible for their suffering? Why do they get sick?

This is a tough question. What I know for sure is that when God created this world, He intended for us to have strong, healthy bodies and freedom from pain and suffering. When evil entered the picture, it brought with it suffering. That is not to say people suffer because of their own personal sins, necessarily, but the world is changed, due to sin being part of the world. Jesus said, "In this world, you will have tribulation."

Just as in the case with Job, I believe that evil forces attack us and cause much suffering in an attempt to get people to blame God and turn away from Him. (Job 2:3-9)

3) God gives us rights as individuals. Because He allows us to choose for ourselves how we'll live, He had to also allow us the freedom to sin. This means He had to allow the consequences of our behaviors, too. Some of those consequences are diseases caused by toxins, accidents caused by risky behaviors, and natural disasters caused by things like changes in the ozone layer, which we have brought about.

4) Though some people think God punishes us by making us suffer, Jesus said that a blind man He healed was born blind, not because of his sin or his parents' sin, but *that the works of God should be revealed in him.*" (John 9:3) God didn't cause the blindness, but He used it to show His power to all who saw Jesus heal the man.

5) Another possible reason God allows suffering is so that our faith in Him will grow, our compassion for others will increase, and we'll be better able to encourage other hurting people (2 Corinthians 1:3-5).

6) Romans 1:22 says that God gives rebellious people over to their own foolishness. He lets us go, hoping that we will return to Him after we hit bottom and see the error of our ways. Giving His permission is not the same as causing the problem. God doesn't cause people to stubbornly refuse to follow His way. He doesn't want us to go ever deeper into degradation, but He does permit us to have our way when we are determined to choose our own path.

But we are not without hope. Though this world is no longer perfect, God will create a perfect world some day in heaven. He will get rid of everything that is not HIS. Suffering, sin, pain, tears and death are not HIS. *"When the perishable has been clothed with the imperishable, and the mortal with immortality, then the saying that is written will come true: 'Death has been swallowed up in victory.'"* (1 Corinthians 15:54)

We have *hope* that all suffering will be relieved when we go to spend eternity with God. But this promise of eternal bliss is only for those who know, serve, and love Him.

God doesn't cause suffering; Satan does. When we get angry at God, it's exactly what Satan wants. By blaming God for evil, we're actually following the one who *is* responsible.

"Be self-controlled and alert. Your enemy the devil prowls around like a roaring lion looking for someone to devour. Resist him, standing firm in the faith, because you know that your brothers throughout the world are undergoing the same kind of sufferings. And the God of all grace, who called you to His eternal glory in Christ, after you have suffered a little while, will Himself restore you and make you strong, firm and steadfast." (1 Peter 5:8-11)

Our souls are of greater importance to God than our bodies are. Though He cares about our physical suffering, healing our soul is more urgent because it is the soul that lives forever. Our relationship with God is what determines where that soul spends eternity. If only those who suffer here on earth would seek God and the true healing (of the soul) that He offers!

In this world, bad things happen to good people. Those who have a personal relationship with God are better able to cope. We can live without fear, even though we do not know what the future holds, if we know the one who holds the future in His hands. When we discover the great love God has for us, we can let go of fear.

Psalm 27:1 says *"The Lord is my salvation. Whom shall I fear?" Jesus triumphed over death, and He alone can save us from eternal death. He can also see us through all the trials of life and bring us safely to heaven.*

As I stated in the beginning pages of this book, I don't have all the answers. I just hope that, in sharing what I've learned through my own experience, I've helped you to feel more at peace knowing God has ultimate control in every circumstance. He is GOOD, no matter what evil befalls us. We can trust in the one who is full of compassion and loves us more than we can imagine. Without that knowledge, I don't know how anyone could cope with the trials of life.

No one can comfort the depths of our sorrows except God. I'm convinced that if you read His promises in the Bible, your heart will be encouraged.

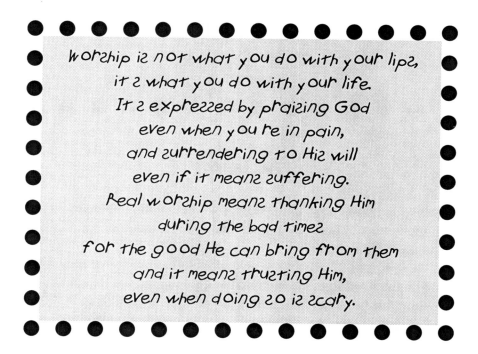

Worship is not what you do with your lips,
it's what you do with your life.
It's expressed by praising God
even when you're in pain,
and surrendering to His will
even if it means suffering.
Real worship means thanking Him
during the bad times
for the good He can bring from them
and it means trusting Him,
even when doing so is scary.

CHAPTER FIVE

THE GAIN OF LOSS

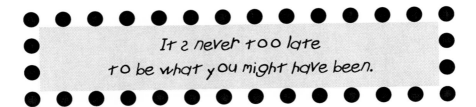

It's never too late
to be what you might have been.

OH, DEER!

Autumn is mating season in the north woods—for the deer that is. It's the season when deer act a little crazy. They become more aggressive than usual.

For instance, last year, a huge buck scared the ear wax out of my grandson and me. We were strolling down our dirt road, minding our own business, when we stumbled upon this "couple." The buck didn't appreciate our interrupting his courtship, and he made sure we knew it. He charged at us, stomping and snorting, with his head down and his horns aimed at my back side. I jerked Cobi's hand and tore out of there like a rat that had accidentally interrupted forty cats at a meeting of Mouseaholics Anonymous. Cobi didn't know grandma could move like that! (I think I exceeded the speed limit.) I was sprinting so fast I didn't even leave footprints, and I yanked poor Cobi's arm with such force that he flew behind me like a cartoon character, dangling horizontally in midair.

Of course, you can't outrun a deer, especially if you're middle aged and 300 pounds overweight. The deer overtook us as we ran, but it veered off at the last second, missing my behind by inches. It galloped past us and bounded into the woods.

We hurried home to change our underwear.

Mating season is also hunting season here in the north woods. That's when some people act a little crazy too. Don't get me wrong. I know there are responsible hunters who practice safety while using a fire arm, but I'm talking about the gun-toting, booze-guzzling folks who swarm to the woods looking for an excuse to party and something to kill.

During hunting season, I can't exercise my dog, walk to my mailbox, or even sit out on my porch for fear of being mortally wounded. Call me paranoid, but a friend of mine was shot while standing in her kitchen talking on the phone. A stray bullet came through her front door, then passed through two interior walls before hitting her in the stomach..

I can imagine how that phone call must have ended. "Oh, sorry to cut you short, but I need to hang up and call 911."

It's not unheard of for hunters to shoot farmers' livestock and the farmers' wives who dare to hang laundry out on the line to dry. Sometimes, they shoot themselves and each other too. I don't care to risk my life by stepping outside when the woods are teaming with killing-crazed sportsmen who don't know a cow or a woman from a white tail deer. It's just my opinion, but I think anyone who can't tell a person from a deer should not be allowed to hunt. I actually know of a man who can't write or drive because he's legally blind, yet he hunts. Gadzooks! You won't catch me walking in the woods while people like that are running loose with loaded guns.

Obviously, I'm not a fan of hunting season, but that's not the only season I hate. I also dread allergy season, flood season, hurricane season, tornado season, football season, monsoon season, and flea and tick season.

The wise king, Solomon, wrote in Ecclesiastes 3 about the seasons of life people go through. There are seasons of happiness and sadness, laughter and tears, war and peace, life and death.

Many people hate the thought of dying; so they refuse to think about that season. They act as if ignoring death will keep the inevitable from happening, but eventually everyone must face the truth that "*it is appointed for men to die.*" (Hebrews 9:27). When that time comes, "*We must all appear before the judgment seat of Christ, so that each one may be recompensed for his deeds in the body, according to what he has done, whether good or bad."* (2 Corinthians 5:10)

Though many fear death, there is no escaping it. No one knows when his time may come, so maybe we should be preparing for it now. We all want to be among those who are ready when they face death. Are you afraid of that season of life, just as I'm afraid of hunting season? It's a question we must each honestly ask ourselves. If you're unsure, you may want to seek the answer in a study of the Scriptures.

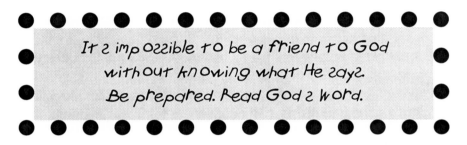

It's impossible to be a friend to God without knowing what He says. Be prepared. Read God's Word.

DEER TRAIL OR EXPRESSWAY?

The husband and I don't take walks together anymore. Our walking styles are too different. He tramps through the woods at a trot while I straggle behind. I'm so busy running to keep up, dodging tree branches and blackberry thorns, tripping over brush, avoiding spider webs, and watching for snakes, that I can't enjoy the "quality time" with my spouse. Hikes through the woods on deer trails are more work than relaxation for me. I prefer a leisurely stroll down a paved road.

While I take the easy road on my daily walks, I know that in other areas of life, taking the easy road can get me into trouble. Jesus said *"Enter through the narrow gate. For wide is the gate and broad is the road that leads to destruction, and many enter through it. But small is the gate and narrow is the road that leads to life and only a few find it."* (Matthew 7:13-14)

I want to travel with those "few" on the narrow road who will end up in heaven, rather than sailing along with the "many" down the expressway that leads in the wrong direction. To those plodding along on the deer trail, folks on the four-lane highway may appear to be enjoying their trip more; but they're going nowhere.

Because it looks quick, easy, and pothole free, the smooth highway seems more carefree than the narrow, rocky trail. People on the wide, easy road aren't often knocked down by the "tree branches" of life and they aren't watching for the "spiders and snakes" of temptation and trials that could catch them unaware. They are, however, in grave danger of reaching the wrong destination.

Though the narrow path leading to life is often difficult, heaven is worth the effort. Because heaven is my goal, I want to find and stay on that narrow road. To do that, I try to obey the commands of Jesus. He said, in John 14:15, "*If you love me, you will keep my commandments.*" Love for Jesus and obedience go together. Obeying Jesus is a demonstration of my love for Him.

How can a person obey the commands of Jesus, if she doesn't know what they are? In the Scriptures, God spelled out what He expects of us. The Bible is our road map for life. Are you following it?

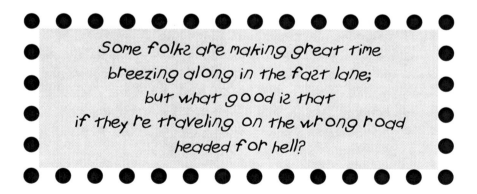

Some folks are making great time
breezing along in the fast lane;
but what good is that
if they're traveling on the wrong road
headed for hell?

PUZZLES AND PLANS

My grandson Cobi used to have trouble putting puzzles together. When he decided a certain piece should fit into a specific spot, there was no convincing him that he could be wrong. No matter how difficult it was to squeeze that piece in, he pushed and pounded on it saying, "It *will* fit!"

How often do we adults act that way when things don't *fit* in our lives? I've heard people say, "I'm going to do what I want, no matter what God wants." I wonder if they realize what they're saying.

According to the Bible, plans that go against God's will don't prosper. *"Unless the LORD builds the house, they labor in vain who build it; unless the LORD guards the city, the watchman keeps awake in vain."* (Psalm 127:1)

The husband and I once fell in love with a gorgeous Victorian home. We wanted to buy that house more than we had ever wanted anything, but it wasn't within our price range. We were determined, so we came up with a plan to get what we wanted. We would get second jobs and take in renters. We would get by with only one car and sell everything else we owned.

We had our plan all figured out, but the house sold to someone else before we could make our offer. We were disappointed at the time, but we later realized it had worked out for the best. We were fortunate that we didn't get what we wanted. We would have been buried in debt forever if we'd bought that house, and we would have eventually regretted the mess we'd gotten into.

We're glad now that God worked out His will instead of letting us have our own way. We've learned that we need to seek God's guidance before making our plans. His plan is always better than our own. Jeremiah 29:11 says, *"I know the plans I have for you, declares the Lord, plans to prosper you and not to harm you, plans to give you hope and a future."*

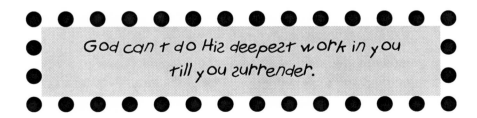

God can't do His deepest work in you
till you surrender.

BUILDING A HOUSE

The husband worked for three years constructing our home. He's a qualified builder, so I trust the house he built.

For my life, I trust the master builder. Since God created life, He knows best how I should live it. He's laid out the blueprint in the Bible.

The most important step in building a house is setting a firm foundation. If a builder takes shortcuts and does a poor job with the foundation, it's pointless to complete the building. It will fall down eventually. Likewise, life crumbles around us if our faith isn't built upon the firm foundation of God's Word and Jesus, the chief cornerstone. The "Rock of Ages" will uphold you and withstand the test of time and the storms of life. Jesus said, *"Only he who does the will of God will live forever."* (Matthew 7:2) He went on to say *"Not everyone who calls me 'Lord' will enter heaven, but only he who does the will of my Father. Many will say to me 'Lord, did we not prophesy in your name and perform miracles?' I will tell them plainly, 'I never knew you.'"*

The second chapter of the book written by James explains, *"A person is justified by what he DOES and not by faith alone."* Since God said it, I believe it. His word is the ultimate authority; it's not a suggestion.

Jesus compared our lives to houses. *"Everyone who hears my words and puts them into practice is like a wise man who builds his house upon rock . . . but everyone who hears my words and does not put them into practice is like a foolish man who builds his house on sand. When the rain comes, the streams rise, the winds blow and beat against the house, and it will fall with a great crash."* (Matthew 7)

What is your life built on?

Building a house by Shaneka S.

your life is the most important
building project you will ever undertake.

The house that Tom built by Kaitlyn Marie

THREE-LEGGED RACES

When you were a kid, did you ever run in three legged races? I loved them and I knew the secret to winning. It was choosing the right partner. If you're going to be tied together, you must be the same size. It's important that your legs are the same length, if you want to run in harmony. Being tied to the right person makes all the difference between winning and losing.

Being tied to the wrong person or the wrong thing can be fatal. Two men once came upon a huge hole in the ground. They wondered how deep it was, so they threw in a few pebbles. They heard no noise, so they threw in some big rocks. Still no noise. "That's REALLY a deep hole," said one. "Throw some bigger rocks down there. Those should make a noise." They threw in a couple of huge rocks and waited. Still nothing.

Then, one of the men dragged a heavy railroad tie to the hole and heaved it in. Not a sound came from the hole. Suddenly, out of the nearby woods, a goat came running like the wind. It rushed past the men and jumped into the hole while the puzzled men just stared.

A farmer came along and asked, "You guys seen my goat?"

"You bet we did!" they said. " It came running like crazy and jumped into this hole!" "Nah." said the farmer, "That couldn't have been *my* goat. My goat was chained to a railroad tie." That unfortunate goat was tied to the wrong thing.

Even the Bible teaches that certain things need to be tied together. Christian faith and good works, for instance. James wrote that faith without works is dead (or powerless) and ineffective. The two must go together. You demonstrate your faith by the way you live. James wrote, *"I will show you my faith by my works."* (James 2:18b)

There are two types of faith. One is head belief, or mentally acknowledging that God is real. You understand certain things about Him and you believe He exists. A lot of people have that sort of faith. The devil even has it. (James 2:19) The Bible says demons believe and shudder.

The other kind of faith is what I call working faith. It's a deep trust in God, believing that He is in charge of your life. Faith like that causes you to act a certain way.

Head belief doesn't impact your life much. But when you deeply believe with all your heart that God is who He says He is and that He's done what He said He would do, then your love for Him is so strong that you're motivated to action. That's dynamic, working faith. It's the faith that is tied to the works you do.

What is your faith tied to?

A man who has faith without deeds
is like a garden with no plants, just seeds.

THE JOY OF SHOPPING

A woman, standing in a checkout line with a heaping shopping cart, told the clerk, "My husband's going to be mad that I've shopped all day." The clerk replied, "I'm sure he'll understand, when you tell him about all the bargains you found." The woman said, "I don't think so. This morning he broke his arm, and he's waiting in the car for me to take him to the emergency room."

Do you lose track of time when sniffing out sales in search of that illusive, ultimate bargain? I sure do. But yesterday, I had a strange experience. I ran into Wal-Mart and bought only the light bulbs I'd gone in for. I was back in my car within ten minutes. Even the husband was shocked.

It's an eerie feeling to shop without a cart, spend less than ten dollars, and leave the store without checking out the sale racks. Normally, I go in for a couple necessities and emerge three hours later with an empty checkbook and a forklift loaded with purchases.

I should win the Nobel prize for shopping. I can turn a trip to the drugstore for toenail clippers into a shopping marathon. I lapse into a half-crazed shopping stupor when I disappear through those automatic doors, and I rarely leave without an overflowing cart full of handy items like the industrial size floor waxer I got for half price, or the duster on a twelve-foot pole—which I've never used—to clean those hard to reach places. (Heck! I don't even clean the *easy* to reach places.)

I've found some great bargains over the years, like those cute little nets you put over your paper plate to keep flies off your potato salad. Too bad I can never find them when we have picnics. Then there were those ten-cent pantyhose. Now that's the sort of discount you don't see every day. I'm sure I'll need them eventually, even if they are iridescent orange and sized for pygmies.

I once picked up some adorable little brushes made especially for cleaning test tubes. I don't have test tubes, but my industrious, obsessive-compulsive husband uses them to scrub light bulbs, door knobs, and loose change.

I was so proud of the wok I got on sale in 1983. I haven't had the chance to use it yet, but last year my clever grandson discovered that it worked well for melting down gold jewelry.

And what about that great deal I got on old Monkees albums? At ninety-eight cents each, they were a steal. Guess what everyone on my Christmas gift list is getting this year?

I'm the poster girl for Shopaholics Anonymous. My drug of choice is the Dollar Store. The last thing the husband shouts as I leave the house is, "Be strong! Stay away from the Dollar Store!" He understands that when it comes to the lure of those treasure-laden aisles, I'm as helpless to resist as a monkey who has sworn off bananas. As I once heard another addict remark, I can have a real shopgasm there. I've been known to push not one but two carts around in that funland. Children follow me and stare in amazement as I load the baskets till their wheels go flat. I stock up on things like lug nuts, nose hair trimmers, hair nets, ear wax remover, para-keet food, and kitty litter. I don't have a cat or a bird; but strays might end up on my doorstep someday, and I'll be prepared. After all, everything in the store is only one dollar, so why not splurge? What a rush! Till I reach the checkout counter and the clerk announces my total of $387.

The husband doesn't understand about sales. He couldn't care less that I saved ten dollars. All he sees are the double digit figures on the receipts. He's so old fashioned, he thinks you shouldn't buy something unless you really need it. I hate the way his lips turn white and form a thin, straight line when he looks through the check register. Then the veins in his neck bulge out and I know he's begin-ning to get peeved with me. That's when I know it's time to lock myself in the bathroom till the storm blows over. I sometimes take six showers a day.

H.M. is a twice-a-year shopper. Every Christmas Eve at 11:00 P.M., he takes his annual five minute dash through the open-all-night drugstore to pick up whatever is on the end of the first two aisles. Family members are always surprised by his unique gifts, like the battery powered tweezers, Power Rangers toothbrush, and the package of Snoopy Band-Aids I received last year.

His second shopping spree takes place during the Vernal Equinox when he spends a total of seven minutes purchasing his new summer wardrobe. He goes into race mode when his feet hit the floor of a store. He never uses a cart and doesn't try anything on. He grabs whatever is nearest the checkout counter. I run to keep up, as he tosses items over my arms.

The next day, I inevitably trudge back to the store and exchange it all because the shoes are three sizes too small and the shirts are size 6X.

I know better than to send H.M. to the grocery store. I once gave him a list with three items on it and he didn't get any of them. Instead of canned tomatoes, he brought home beets. I got a bag of flour instead of sugar; and rather than picking up oranges, he bought a case of grapefruit. We HATE grapefruit. He says he makes mistakes like these because he doesn't read labels. Always being in a hurry, he simply grabs whatever looks like the item he's after. I think he does it on purpose so I won't send him to the store again.

Maybe I should be a little more like him, though. Think of the time I would save if I spent less of it in search of that ultimate bargain.

Actually, I don't need to shop at all to find the deal of the century. I've already found it—and not just the deal of this century, but of every century.

The best deal ever has been called "the pearl of great price" (Matthew 13:45) which is worth everything you can sell to buy it. It's a deal God made two thousand years ago. He paid a ransom for you with the life of His only son. It purchased your freedom from the power of sin and death.

The blood of Jesus bought eternal life for every person who is willing to accept His gift. You won't find a greater deal in any mall on earth.

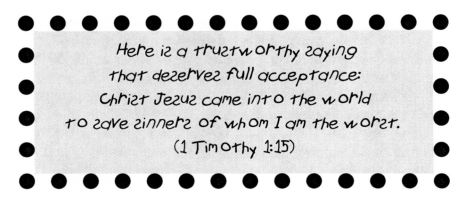

Here is a trustworthy saying
that deserves full acceptance:
Christ Jesus came into the world
to save sinners of whom I am the worst.
(1 Timothy 1:15)

OUT OF THE ASHES

Three days after the September 11 tragedy, rescue workers dug five firefighters out of the ashes of what used to be the World Trade Center Towers. These fortunate men, who survived when so many others perished, were unable to get out of the debris on their own. Clinging to hope, they were powerless in the darkness under the rubble. They counted on others to free them and bring them out into the light so they could return to their lives.

Many of us are also buried in the dark under the wreckage of past failures. We cling to hope in the lonely darkness and wait for someone to rescue us, bringing us into the light and back to our lives.

Sin ensnares us. Like those trapped firefighters, we're lost in the rubble that sin makes of our lives. Like them, we're counted among the dead. That is, until Jesus rescues us. Freeing us from the ash heap of our past, He brings us into the light and gives us a new life.

Do you feel trapped in the ashes of your past? Jesus is your rescuer. Psalm 50:15 says: *"Call upon Me in the day of trouble; I shall rescue you, and you will honor Me."*

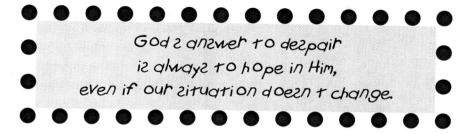

God z anzwer to dezpair
iz alwayz to hope in Him,
even if our zituation doezn't change.

WHAT'S INSIDE?

I offered the teens in my Sunday School class a tray of caramel-covered apples. Jon chose the largest one with the most nuts and took a big bite."Yuck!" he yelled as he spit it out. "That's no apple. It's a big onion!" I think Jon learned the lesson: No matter how the outside looks, it's what's inside that counts. Our society focuses on outward appearances. We can easily get caught up in trying to look good to others. But sometimes we look great on the outside and harbor all kinds of not so great stuff inside, like pride, bitterness, resentment, and arrogance. These are opposites of the humble attitude God desires.

Bad attitudes can make our good deeds meaningless. According to the Bible, you can give away all you possess and even sacrifice your life; but it profits you nothing, if your attitude isn't right. (1 Corinthians 13:3)

You may outdo everyone in the good works department, but that won't earn you an entrance ticket to heaven. You can never be good enough to deserve God's love. Appearing righteous doesn't lead you closer to Him. It's the unseen, hidden matters of the heart (known only to Him) that God cares about. *The Lord does not look at the things man looks at. Man looks at the outward appearance, but the Lord looks at the heart.* (I Samuel 16:7)

Good deeds, church work, and perfect attendance can't replace a relationship with God. He's not impressed by how good your life appears. It's a change of your heart that He yearns for.

Even though King David committed murder and adultery, God said David was a man after His own heart. God could say that because He looked at David's attitude and into his heart's intentions. He knew David was humble and wanted to do right. This is what David wrote, after Nathan the prophet rebuked him for his sin: *"Have mercy on me, O God, according to your unfailing love; according to your great compassion, blot out my transgressions. Wash away all my iniquity and cleanse me from my sin. For I know my transgressions, and my sin is always before me. Against you, you only, have I sinned and done what is evil in your sight, so that you are proved right when you speak and justified when you judge."* (Psalm 51)

David was truly sorry for his sins and genuinely desired to change his ways and please God. His repentant attitude mattered more to God than what David had done.

How can you tell whether you have a humble, repentant heart like David's? Here is the acid test: Those who are truly repentant don't care if they lose the respect of the entire world, as long as they make things right with God. They are glad when their sin is exposed, so it can be dealt with. Instead of justifying or covering up sin, a repentant person will throw himself on the mercy of God.

True repentance is the result of godly sorrow (2 Corinthians 7:10). This means understanding that sins hurt God and wanting to change in order to please Him. A repentant person will be thankful to the one who exposed his sin, even if it caused him pain. He will also be willing to make restoration to those he has hurt.

When God looks within our hearts, He sees who we really are. By outward appearances, we may look like good people, but it's what's inside that matters most.

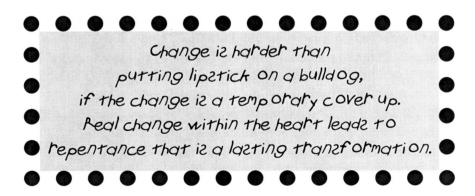

Change is harder than putting lipstick on a bulldog, if the change is a temporary cover up. Real change within the heart leads to repentance that is a lasting transformation.

IT'S NOT MY FAULT!

I'm built like the cab of a Mack truck, but it's not my fault. I inherited an overabundance of fat cells that constantly scream for foods fried in axle grease or covered with chocolate sauce. My ancestors passed on to me a family gene that renders me powerless to resist anything doused in sugar or laden with fat. Yeah, that's it. It's all in my genes. My family is to blame!

My urge to devour a two-pound bag of Fritos while typing at the computer is totally out of my control. It's probably due to some tragic accident I had at a young age in a cornfield . . . the memory of which I have since repressed.

I hate to cook, but that's not my fault either. I must have experienced an early life trauma involving a stove. And my short temper can be blamed on my Irish heritage.

Window washing and stove cleaning are two other things I hate to do. Hmmmm. That must be my mother's fault somehow. Maybe she made me clean my room too often when I was a kid. It certainly CAN'T be that I'm just plain lazy. Nothing, you see, is MY fault. I was a middle child. That's a good excuse.

I guess it's human nature to make excuses for our behavior, and some of us carry it to an extreme. We don't like to take responsibility for our own choices.

A fugitive once hid for three cold nights in a forest to elude police. When he was arrested, doctors had to amputate his frostbitten toes. He later told reporters, "If the detective had done his job properly, he would've caught me sooner and I wouldn't have frozen my toes." He even threatened to sue. He said, "If I'd been in jail, where I belonged, I wouldn't have lost my toes."

We tend to blame others for our own bad choices. Unfaithful husbands blame their wives, delinquents blame their parents, employees blame bosses, patients blame doctors, students blame teachers; and if all other excuses fail, we can say, "The devil made me do it!"

Why is it so difficult to admit our mistakes?

Denying, minimizing, or justifying them can wreak havoc with relationships and our health. In Psalm 32, the Bible says, *"When I kept silent about my sin, my body wasted away. I groaned all day long. My vitality was drained away."*

Hiding sin often causes more pain than owning up to the truth, but admitting our wrongs brings healing. It heals physical ailments brought on by the stress, and it heals relationships with other people. It also heals our most important relationship—with God.

"If we claim to be without sin, we deceive ourselves and the truth is not in us . . . If we claim we have not sinned, we make God out to be a liar." (1 John 1:8 and 10) We have the chance to bring peace into our hearts when we get real, repent and draw near to God.

When we leave our old way of life and turn to God, we leave guilt and shame behind. What a relief to have a clear conscience! Admitting our wrongdoing, confessing it to God, and turning from it will lead us in a new direction for a better life.

"You do not delight in sacrifice. Otherwise, I would give it. You are not pleased with burnt offerings. The (pleasing) sacrifices of God are a broken (humble) spirit; a broken and contrite heart, Oh, God, you will not despise." (Psalm 51:16, 17)

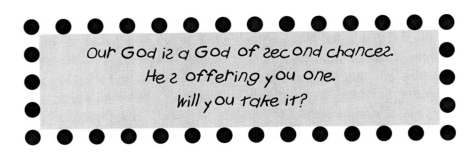

Our God is a God of second chances.
He's offering you one.
Will you take it?

U-TURN

I was driving with the husband when we approached a fork in the road. Confused about the quickest route to our destination, I asked, "Does it matter which road I take?" Trying to be funny, he chuckled, "Not to me, it doesn't." But the direction we choose and the road we take DOES matter. It determines where we end up. If I want to go to New York, I don't board a train headed for Chicago.

Likewise, the direction we choose for our lives matters too. Sometimes we don't consciously choose a certain path; but when we avoid one direction, we're automatically aimed in the opposite direction. Imagine a kid playing hooky who stays as far away from the school as he can get. He could end up lost, not because he chooses that route, but because he's concerned with where he doesn't want to go, rather than paying attention to where he is going.

Similarly, people who choose the road to wealth and power, which requires that they invest all their energies in earning money, often find that they've left behind the road leading to intimate relationships.

Sometimes people get caught up in a certain lifestyle and find themselves doing things totally out of character. No one wakes up one morning and decides he wants to become a drug addict or alcoholic and give up his health, relationships, money, and self worth. I doubt that there's a person alive who deliberately chooses to devote his life to an addictive substance. He changes slowly over time; and without really noticing, he becomes a different person.

The man who breaks into his first house doesn't intend to become a lifetime thief. A passionate teen never wants to get pregnant. They think they'll just have a little fun. In reality *"after desire has conceived, it gives birth to sin; and sin, when it is full-grown, gives birth to death."* (James 1:14-16)

It's like a frog in a pot on the stove. As the water gradually gets hotter, the frog doesn't notice the temperature rising. He stupidly sits there in the pot, instead of jumping out to safety. He ends up being Wednesday night's supper because he didn't realize he was even on the menu!

Like the frog, we can be oblivious to the hot water we're in. We often don't realize how far we've traveled in the wrong direction till we stop and remember from where we came. One day we wake up and wonder how we got off track and into the soup.

At some point in each of our lives, we need to take a reality check and ask, "Am I headed in a direction I never intended to go? Do I need to make a U-turn?"

People came from everywhere to hear John the Baptist preach. He told them the Messiah was soon to appear and they'd better get ready to meet Him. John told them their hearts were not prepared because they were still holding onto their sins. He said, *"outside you appear clean and holy, but inside you're full of dead men's bones."* He warned them that they must deal with their sin before they could believe in the savior. John told people they needed to repent and turn to God, then do works that showed repentance (Acts 26:20).

According to the Bible, one reason Jesus came to earth was to call all men everywhere to repent (Acts 17:30). Repentance is mentioned more than 100 times in the Bible. Seems to be pretty important, so I want to be sure I understand this word.

The words "repent" and "turn" are used by Bible translators interchangeably. The idea is to have a change of heart. John did not call the people just to be sorry, but to change their attitudes and lifestyles.

The word repent literally means "to do an about face," or to "go in the other direction." Picture someone stopping in the middle of the road to listen for God's voice, then going in the direction God wants, rather than the direction he chose for himself. God instructs us to turn around, not because He's a dictator who wants to control us like puppets, but because He wants to lead us away from disaster.

Jesus preached that we must leave our dead end roads and break out of the rut leading to destruction. He said, *"Unless you repent, you too will all perish."* (Luke 13:3b)

Once we realize our need to change direction, how do we know which way to turn? If we turn from our own ways to just another of man's ways, we only set our course down another futile path. Jesus said, *"Can a blind man lead a blind man? Will they not both fall into a pit?"* (Luke 6:39) Instead, we need to learn God's will and turn to that. *"Be very careful, then, how you live . . . do not be foolish, but understand what the Lord's will is."* (Ephesians 5:15-17)

Is the direction of your life pleasing to God? Are you on the path He planned for your life? (Psalm 16:11) The only way to travel is in God's will. *"Turn to me and be saved . . . for I am God, and there is no other."* (Isaiah 35:22) Don't drift through life so caught up in the motion that you forget to watch where you're heading. Let God point you in the right direction.

The New Testament is filled with verses about the turn around called repentance. Here are a few to consider:

1 Peter 3:10: *"Let him who means to love life and see good days . . . turn away from evil and do good."*

Acts 17:30 *"In the past, God overlooked ignorance; but now He commands all people everywhere to repent."*

2 Tim 2:19 *"The Lord knows those who are His," and "everyone who confesses the name of the Lord must turn away from wickedness."*

James 5:19-20 (Phi) *"My brothers, if any of you should wander away from the truth and another should turn him back onto the right path, then the latter may be sure that in turning a man back from his wandering course he has rescued a soul."*

2 Cor 7:8-10 (Phi) *". . . I can see now that my letter upset you, though only for a time; and now I am glad I sent it, not because I want to hurt you but because it made you grieve for things that were wrong. In other words, the result was to make you sorry, as God would have had you sorry . . . . The sorrow that God uses means a change of heart."*

We can be obstinate and hardheaded.
Jesus confronts us with a choice:
Repent from the lifestyle that hurts God
or reap the consequences of rejecting him.
He allows no middle ground.
The life we live in response to the message of
Jesus has enormous consequence.
He died for us. How can we refuse to change
our hearts and live to follow Him?

CHAPTER SIX

TRIUMPH iN TRIALS

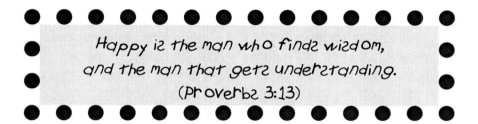

Happy iz the man who findz wizdom,
and the man that getz underztanding.
(Proverbz 3:13)

THE ROAD OF LiFE

Have you noticed that vacations rarely go the way you planned? Here's a typical scenario: Mom and dad outline a fun and interesting trip for the family. They excitedly pack the Volkswagon and pull out of the driveway with great expectations. Then five miles down the road, a crazy driver cuts dad off in traffic, mom spills her Doctor Pepper in her lap, an albatross splatters a five gallon bucket of poop on the windshield, and somebody in the backseat spews chunks on the carpet, seat, and little sister. These are telltale signs that the trip isn't going to be what you'd anticipated.

When I flew across the country last year, I lost my driver's license in the airport. For the safety of other passengers, it's essential that everyone have a photo ID. I didn't have one. Apparently I looked like a terrorist, so the stewardess wouldn't let me on the plane. Security people were called to the scene and they pondered what to do with me. They finally decided to allow me on, if I passed a thorough body and luggage search.

When I say "thorough," that's just what I mean. I not only had to take everything out of my suitcase (including my dirty underwear) and then try to squeeze it back in again; but I had to take off my shoes and socks and even unzip my pants and roll down the elastic of my underwear. These were not things I'd planned as part of the trip—especially not in front of a hundred other passengers. What a humiliating predicament. Remember this story when you travel – and remember your mother's admonition to always wear clean undies when you leave the house. You never know who might see them.

Another trip that didn't go according to plans was a short, three hour outing with my brother and sister (kind of like the three hour trip of the SS Minnow on *Gilligan's Island*). Our car broke down in a snow storm and we had to spend a day and a night in a motel. This might not have been too bad if we'd had enough money to get separate rooms or if we'd brought luggage with us. We had no change of clothes or even a toothbrush (ewww)! The three of us slept in one room and one of us—I won't mention any names—snored loudly all night, keeping the other two awake.

My sister considered wrapping the telephone cord around my neck to strangle me as I slept, while my brother searched the dresser drawers just in case a previous occupant may have left a roll of duct tape. When they threatened to perform a tracheotomy on me, I decided to stay awake and sit up in the chair the rest of the night. That wasn't how any of us had expected the trip to go.

Mishaps, break downs, accidents, illnesses, injuries, unexpected side trips. That's a picture of our journey through life. Trouble is around every corner. Believers know there's a great destination for us at the end of the road, but the trip can be horrendous.

When I became a Christian, I thought I had it made and the trip would be an easy one. Life was good and it would only get better. I had not heard of life mapping at that time; but if I had mapped out my life back then, the map would have been a straight line shooting right up to heaven with no bumps and curves.

Boy, was I misinformed! It took me about forty eight hours to discover that my expectations were unrealistic and it wasn't going to be such easy sailing after all.

Nobody's life is a bowl of apricots. In fact, it can often be more like the pits, even for Christians. Life doesn't go smoothly because you're saved. You still have to maneuver the potholes.

The Bible says the truth will set you free. When you accept the truth that life ain't fair, things get somewhat easier because you're not stunned by the detours.

The road of life is sometimes an arduous crawl uphill and sometimes you're speeding downhill, awaiting the crash. Think of the wilderness wanderings of the Israelite people. They were all over the place during their 40 years in the dessert. When they complained, Moses told them, *"Do not fear, stand by and see the salvation of the Lord which He will accomplish for you. The Lord will fight for you while you keep silent."*

I have a hard time with that last part about keeping silent. I'm not the silent type. I'm more like the nagging, cranky, loudmouth, bossy type. (But after all, I AM the smartest woman I know and others need to benefit from my wisdom, don't they?)

I'm a master complainer. I don't need to look very hard to find something to whine about. When the Israelites complained, it was about things like not enough water and not enough food. I may not complain about those same things, but my whining springs from the same sort of attitude. I forget that God is not only great and powerful and loving and merciful, but that's He's WITH me. My memory is nonexistent, but my forgetter works great, so I need to be reminded quite often that I'm not alone on this journey.

I'm glad God is my ever present navigator, because I couldn't handle this trip over life's bumpy roads on my own.

Whatever you have learned or received
or heard from me,
or seen in me put it into practice.
And the God of peace will be with you.
(Philippians 4:9)

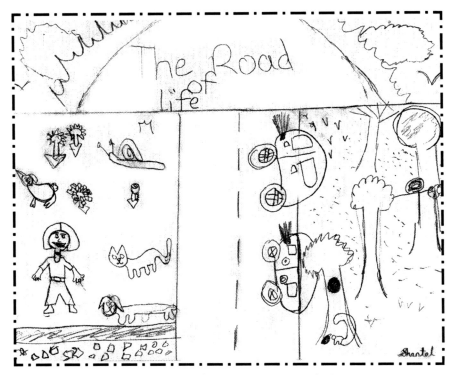

Road of life by Shantel S.

EXTREME MAKEOVER

The husband and I are "boat people." Not the kind that fled from Viet Nam. We're the kind of boat people who drive half a day to wait in line for an hour at the boat landing, just to take a thirty minute boat ride.

H.M. is actually more of a boat person than I am. Having nearly drowned in a high school swimming class, I don't much like water and could live without setting foot in it except that I must shower occasionally. In fact, I'm uncomfortable near any body of water unless it has a drain and a faucet.

The husband has spent nearly as much of his life in water as he's spent on land. He's so impassioned with restoring antique wood boats that he can't resist a rotted hull any more than a hemorrhoid sufferer can resist Preparation H.

160

When I look at a dilapidated boat, I see peeling paint, rusted chrome, and rotted wood. The husband, however, envisions the boat's previous splendor and the magnificent treasure that it will be after he's worked his magic. He gets more excited than a squirrel in a peanut warehouse, and he can hardly wait to begin restoring his treasure to perfection.

I think that's how God is with us. He sees what we're made of; but He also knows how much better we can be, if we allow Him to renovate us from the inside out. Just as the husband can't wait to refinish a boat, God is eager to perfect each of His people. Unfortunately, we're not always eager to let Him. We're content to remain as we are. That is, until life falls apart. Usually, it is only then that we soften, becoming compliant and changeable.

Boats that come into the husband's shop for rejuvenation look aged, battle scarred, and worn out. Yet, they're never beyond repair.

He must often gut entire sections that have rotted. With tender care, he reconstructs them. He replaces missing parts, overhauls the engine, and refinishes the chrome.

The last step in the restoration process is to painstakingly apply layer upon layer of varnish. He sands and polishes it to produce a smooth finish in which he can see his reflection. In a matter of months, he transforms old wrecks into trophy winners. It's possible because he's a craftsman who knows what he's doing.

People can also be reconstructed by a master craftsman. Who better than our creator could transform our brokeness? Even renovations that seem impossible become glorious possibilities with the master's skillful touch.

Have you felt like a battered old boat, beaten by the waves and rocks of life? Have you suffered abuse and neglect like a peeling, rotted hull? Are you weary and no longer able to stay afloat in the sea of adversity? Maybe, like an antique boat, you need a restoration.

God wants to remove from your heart the decayed parts affected by bitterness, selfishness, unforgiveness, or other sins. Just as the husband is compelled to undertake boat projects, because he's anxious to see what they can become, God is eager to see His purpose for you completed. His goal is a total makeover, and He will persevere until he's renovated your heart. If you don't resist His makeover, you'll become like Him. Then, like the new finish of a renovated wood boat, you will reflect the image of the one who restored you.

Though God loves you just as you are, He can't leave you that way any more than the husband can turn away from an old weathered boat. H.M. has a gift for recognizing what's worn out but precious, and making it new again. God also recognizes the value of his precious children, and He lovingly offers us a new life.

Will you allow His masterful touch to restore your heart?

Change is inevitable,
except from vending machines.

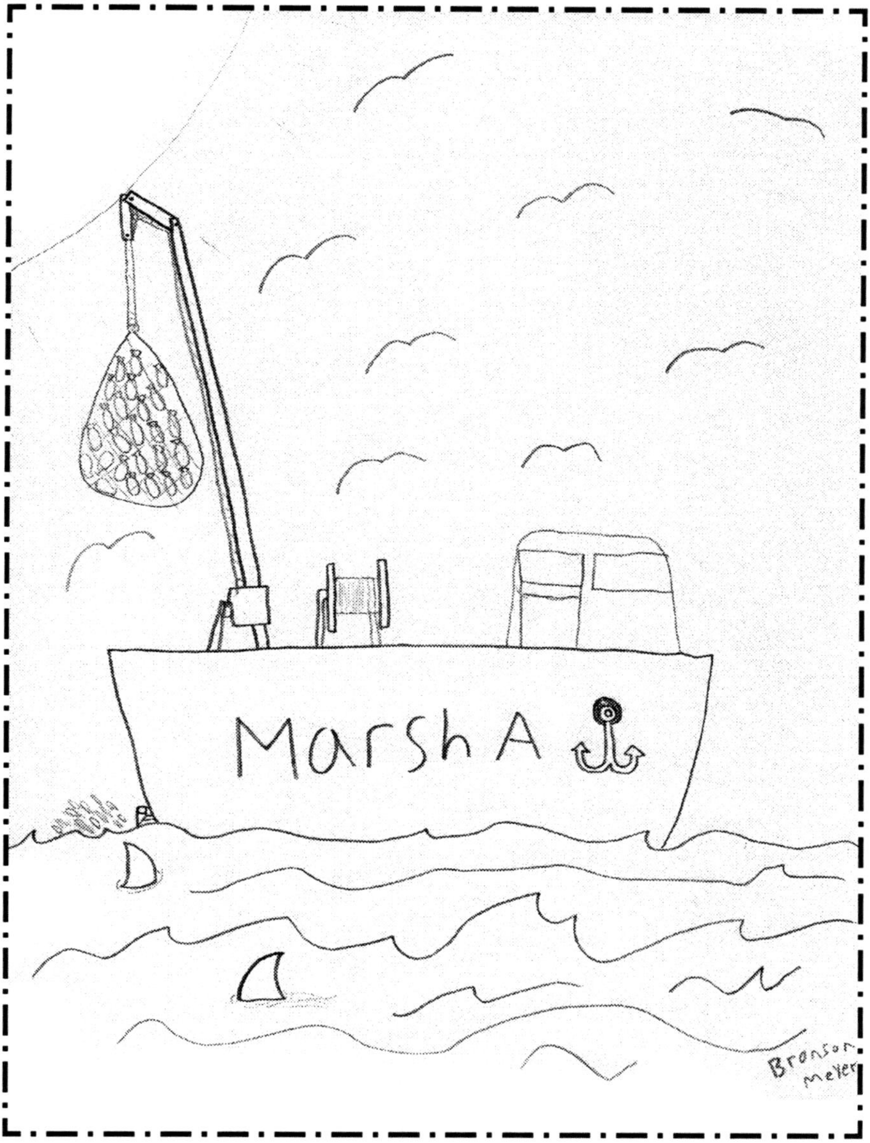
MarshA
Bronson Meyer

Boat by Bronzon M.

FAST FORWARD

Do you sometimes wish life were like a VCR so you could fast forward through the bad parts? Life often doesn't go quite the way
we've planned it. We can usually expect the unexpected, and it can
be devastating. Cars and washing machines break down, computers
and air planes crash, youthful beauty and bank accounts dry up. We
lose jobs and hair. Tires and chests go flat, marriages and bodies fall
apart, jobs and friendships end, people disappoint us, children get
sick, and loved ones leave us. Suffering is inescapable, so wouldn't
it be great to speed through the unpleasantness? I used to wish that
the weekends would hurry and get here. The husband said I was
wishing my life away. For once, he was right (but only that one
time).

When we're young, we can't wait to be old enough to drive a
car, buy a house, or get married.When we get older, we realize how
fast time passes, and then we wish we could slow it down. We lose
our youth too soon. And along with it, we lose our teeth, our hair,
and our memories.

The days of our lives go by more swiftly than a weaver's shut-
tle, according to Job 9:25 & 26. *"They are swifter than a runner.
They pass by like swift ships, like an eagle swooping on its prey."*

James 4:14 says life is like a vapor that *"appears for a little
time and then vanishes away."* Unfortunately, we can't push the
"pause" button to slow life down. No matter what our birth dates,
we're each speeding toward old age at an alarming rate. That's why
it's never too soon to begin preparing for eternity.

What was written in earlier times
was written for our instruction,
so that through perseverance
and the encouragement of the Scriptures
we might have hope.

PROFOUND QUESTION

"How do you feel when people are mean to you?" I asked. It was one of those rare "teachable moments." My five year old grandson and I were sitting on the porch swing, enjoying a warm spring day. I had his undivided attention (or so I thought), so I seized the opportunity to discuss a subject I'd been wanting to bring up at just the right time.

"I don't like it," was his predictable reply—just what I'd hoped he would say. I explained that others feel that same way when he's unkind to them.

To my delight, he seemed to be listening for a change. He pursed his lips and stared at me in silence with wide eyes.

"If you don't share your toys with other boys, they will feel sad," I continued. Cobi appeared to concentrate on my words, ruminating over them like a cow chewing its cud.

"And if you don't take turns on the swing, other kids might not want to play with you." He squinted his eyes, wrinkled his brow, and scratched his head. I knew he was soaking up my wisdom like a sponge. I was thrilled that he didn't respond with the usual arguments like, "But graaaaaaama, when I tripped Robert, he didn't get hurt, " or "Haley likes it when I take her ball."

Pleased with myself and the way my lecture was going, I summed it up with the golden rule. "We need to treat other people the same way we like to be treated," I explained. "That way, things will go more smoothly and everyone will be happier." Satisfied that I had conveyed this important lesson to him, and that he'd taken it so well, I concluded my discourse by asking if he had any questions.

"Yeah," he replied enthusiastically. "Why don't bugs have ears, and do they ever sneeze?"

Marsha Jordan

Bug by Elizabeth S.

The laughter of a child is the light of a house.
(An African Proverb)

166

I LOVE TO CAMP-NOT!

I'll never understand the phenomena of camping. I tried it once for a few hours, and that was enough for me. I vowed never to do it again and I've had no trouble keeping that promise.

I'm not an outdoorsy person. I don't care to go on hikes unless an escalator is involved. And wearing the same underwear for three days because I forgot to pack more just isn't for me. Though I love sunshine and fresh air, I can enjoy them from my recliner next to the window. And there are only two kinds of greenery I like: The kind I can eat and the kind I can spend. I'd rather take in the scenery of a mall than a wilderness trail. I prefer to watch for sales, not snakes and deer droppings. Roughing it, to me, means having a broken TV remote or staying in a hotel without a pool.

Why would anyone leave their comfy bed to sleep on the cold, hard ground? It takes a special sort of person to do that. By special I mean someone who is not the brightest flame in the camp fire. Some people will even pay hard-earned money just so they can leave their cozy home, warm shower, and air conditioning. All this to cook hot dogs on a stick, cover their bodies with stinky, cancer-causing insecticide, and squeeze a family of cranky kids and a large drooling dog into a one-man, bug-infested, leaky tent. Then they lie awake shivering in the rain and swatting bloodthirsty mosquitoes the size of blue-footed boobie birds.

The husband once took our son on a camping adventure in the back yard. The kid was disappointed when he learned there were no video games or stereo in the tent and the sleeping bag had only one temperature setting, which was brain-frying hot.

The son made it through half the night. At 2:00 a.m., he decided mom had the right idea. (She's not as dumb as she looks.) He snuck into the house and crawled into his bed, leaving dad to continue the adventure alone.

The following night, the abandoned tent looked a little forlorn standing alone in our backyard; but it didn't stay empty for long.

A hungry bear strolled inside, apparently lured by the enticing smell of bits of hot dog, bun crumbs, and burnt marshmallow remains stuck to a paper plate. The rude bear didn't have manners enough to exit the tent by the same door he entered. Instead, he created a back door and ripped his way out. This is one more reason I do not camp. I refuse to share my sleeping quarters with anything hairier than the husband.

To me, camping is not a vacation. A real vacation is lounging by the pool at a five star hotel and having breakfast delivered to me in bed around noonish. That's the life for me! I like to be pampered. That's why I'm looking forward to heaven. (The other reason is that I want to spend eternity in the nonsmoking section.)

I would be very surprised if there were campgrounds in heaven. I'm certain there won't be snakes, outhouses, or ostrich-size vampire bugs. No deer flies, horse flies, or black flies. No ticks, bats, or over-crowded, leaking tents. No greasy repellent, hot dog sticks, or hungry bears.

Jesus said, *"In My Father's house are many mansions; if it were not so, I would have told you; for I go to prepare a place for you."* (John 14:2) I can handle living in a mansion. That's just my style. I hope it's a big Victorian mansion lavishly decorated with rare antiques. Yeah, I can picture myself there. I'm glad Jesus is preparing a place for me!

Camping by Kaitlyn

CAMPING ADVICE

If you're the type of person who believes camping is a little bit of heaven on earth, here are some tips to guarantee a pleasant experience for you:

1) When hiking, you will stay warm in cool weather and cool in warm weather if you wear layers of clothes that breathe. However, avoid clothing that pants, passes gas, or burps the National Anthem.

2) Wear clothing with long sleeves. Sleeves not only protect you from sunburn and keep mosquitoes and ticks off your skin, they also come in handy if you forgot to bring Kleenex or toilet paper.

3) Campground too crowded? Ensure your privacy and guarantee that nobody will camp too close by playing a tuba every

morning and evening. It's also helpful to place a set of drums or a Rottweiler outside your tent.

4) When cooking over an open fire, toss a few potatoes into the coals. After an hour, they make a great high-fiber meal that sticks to the ribs. You can carry some in your backpack for on-the-trail snacks. If you forget to take them out of the fire after an hour, that's okay. You can still use them as foot warmers in your sleeping bag or throw them at your snoring spouse.

5) If you forget your pork and beans or Dinty Moore beef stew, feast on fresh game instead. No gun? No problem. Make a sling shot from the elastic in your boxer shorts and use it to fling those petrified taters.

6) Suspend any leftover food high in a tree where bears can't steal it. If you don't have leftovers to tie up, find another use for the string. You could make a snare to catch your next meal, or use it to tie up that snoring tent mate.

7) Staying warm in a cold tent can be a problem. I've found it helpful to place a hot pizza in your sleeping bag, but be careful. The sauce can get messy. If you happen to have a hairy back, then rolling over onto the pizza can work to your advantage.

After the cheese has cooled, ripping it off your back quickly works just as well as a bikini wax.

And one final warning. I read this on the Internet, and no author was noted. Therefore I don't know who gets the credit for this, but it's good advice: In Alaska, tourists are warned to wear tiny bells on their clothing when hiking in bear country. The bells scare away *most* bears. Tourists are also cautioned to watch the ground on the trail, paying particular attention to bear droppings to be alert for the presence of Grizzly Bears. One can tell a Grizzly dropping because it has tiny bells in it.

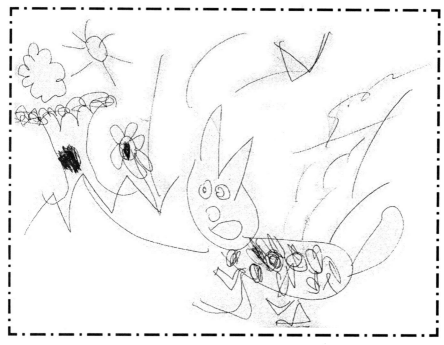

Bear by Meghan J.

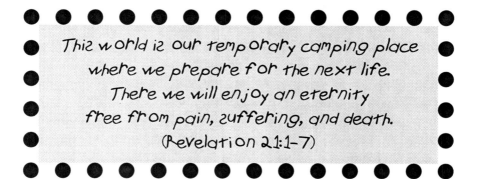

This world is our temporary camping place
where we prepare for the next life.
There we will enjoy an eternity
free from pain, suffering, and death.
(Revelation 21:1-7)

DEAD MEN WALKING

Lazarus had been dead and rotting in the grave for days. His sister told Jesus, *"He stinketh."* (And who says there's no humor in the Bible?) But Jesus called Lazarus out of the grave.

When He came upon a funeral procession, Jesus raised that man to life, too. Then there was the little girl he brought back to life. She had died only moments before Jesus arrived at her home.

Which of these three people was more dead? Lazarus had been dead the longest and smelled the worst, so would you say that he was the "deadest?" No, there are no degrees. Dead is dead.

It's the same way with sin. A sinner is a sinner, period. Sinners are law breakers. They've broken God's laws and their own moral laws. All sinners look the same to God. Because He's perfect and just, God can't have anything to do with sin. Sin separates us from Him.

Sin is a killer. Whether it's the sin of murder or just a little lie, the result is the same. It kills relationships.

Like death, sin has no degrees. Wrong is wrong and we've all done wrong. No one is better or worse than anybody else. We've all missed the mark or goal God had in mind for us.

Check out the list in Galatians 5:19-23. It includes behaviors like jealousy, outbursts of anger, and envy. Who isn't guilty of these? We're all in the same sinking boat, and we need a lifeline. According to the Bible, all who sin (or fall short of what God expects) will earn the wages of their actions, which is spiritual death (Romans 6:23). That's eternal separation from God. Our sins have grieved the One who created and loved us. They've put up a barrier between us. We are dead to God in the same way that a family may say of a relative, "He is dead to me."

We are like walking dead people. We "stinketh" and we need a new life. But there's hope, because Jesus built a bridge to span the separation between God and people. He made it possible for us to be raised (spiritually) and "walk in a new life." This new life begins when we become Christians. (John 3:3 and 1Peter 1:23) How can we know for sure that we have been "born again" to this new life? Opinions vary, but only one opinion matters. That's God's.

Some folks say, "I'm a good person and I do good things, so that makes me a Christian." But don't many Muslims, Buddhists, and even atheists do good things? Doing good doesn't make you a Christian (Romans 3:20). And the Bible clearly says that nobody could ever be good enough to work his way to heaven, anyway. "*There is no one righteous, not even one.*" (Romans 3:10).

Some believe that because they attend church every week, they must be Christians. But if I spend each Sunday in my garage, does that mean I'm a car? If I take my dog to church every week, does that make him a Christian? People of many denominations attend their worship services regularly, but they are not all Christians; so attending church doesn't mean you're a Christian. In fact, the Bible even refers to people who worship God in vain. Apparently attending weekly worship services can actually be a waste of your time, if your heart isn't right. (Matthew 15:9)

Where does that leave us? It takes more than going through certain motions, knowing certain religious facts, or attending the correct church to be in good standing with God and saved from the consequences of sin. In Matthew 7, Jesus said that not everyone who calls Him "Lord" will get to heaven. On judgment day, He will say to many, "*Away from me. I never knew you.*"

To cross the chasm that separates us from God, the dividing wall must be removed. Our guilt must be erased so we'll be seen as righteous in God's sight. Hebrews 9:14 says, "*The Blood of Christ cleanses our consciences*" and "*without the shedding of blood there is no forgiveness.*"

Jesus provided the way to wipe out our guilt and make us righteous. We can be forgiven and not held accountable to pay the penalty for our crimes.

When Jesus died, he paid the price that we owed for our unrighteousness (sin). Jesus is the bridge spanning the canyon between God and us. Through Jesus, we may connect again with our creator and be right with Him once more. Salvation without Jesus is not possible. (John 14:6)

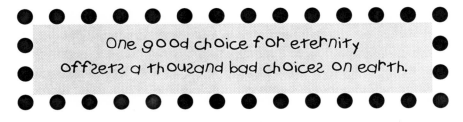

One good choice for eternity
offsets a thousand bad choices on earth.

CROSSING THE CHASM

Jesus provided the gift of atonement, but not everyone accepts His gift. Some don't want the gift, but many just don't know how to receive it.

The first step across the chasm between us and God is believing that Jesus was who He said He was—the Christ.

The next step is repentance. You've probably heard about repentance, especially if you watch television. The word may call to mind an excited preacher with slicked back hair and a shiny suit. He was probably thumping on his Bible and shouting, "Repent!" Though most of us are familiar with that word, many don't know its real meaning. Repentance does not mean sorrow. It means "change."

Mark Twain said, "The only person who likes change is a wet baby." It seems natural to resist change, but change is necessary or there is no repentance. One cannot claim "I believe in Jesus, so I'm okay." (Remember that the devil also believes, but he's certainly not okay in God's sight.) A change of heart and attitude is essential.

Jesus said, *"Repent, for the kingdom of heaven is near."* (Matthew 4:17) Repentance involves being sorry for past mistakes and making the effort to turn away from them. A repentant heart causes me to look at things differently and to desire a new way of life that will please God.

The truth will set you free, but it often makes you miserable first. Let's say you've discovered the truth that, just like every living person, you have sinned and hurt God. Your sin has separated you from Him. When you accept the truth that you've disappointed God, you will most likely feel sorry that you've broken your relationship with Him. This sorrow is referred to in the Bible as "godly" sorrow, and Paul wrote that it is a good thing, which leads to even better things. (2 Corinthians 7:7-11) Godly sorrow isn't how you feel when you wish you hadn't been caught doing wrong. It's not being sorry that you must face the consequences of your actions. It's being heart broken that you've hurt God, and it's wanting to change so you won't hurt Him any more.

In the last section of the passage in 2 Corinthians 7, it says, *"Godly sorrow brings repentance that leads to salvation and leaves no regret."* Note that it doesn't say repentance equals salvation. It leads to it.

Godly sorrow, then, will lead to a change of attitude. It will cause us to admit our sins and ask forgiveness. It will make us want to invite God into our lives and give Him control of how we live. Godly sorrow will make us ask God to change our hearts so we will want what He wants and think like He thinks. It will cause us to want God to abide with us. It will lead us to ask Jesus to live within our hearts and help us make better choices.

This whole process is repentance—the act of spiritually turning away from our old lives toward a whole new life in Christ.

True repentance involves accepting Jesus as SAVIOR. Few people will argue about their need for a savior, but repentance also involves asking God to be LORD and MASTER. This is where many people stop short. It's one thing to let a savior remove your guilt. It's another thing to surrender control over to your master. True repentance is demonstrated by turning your life over to God.

It is said that two things are certain,
death and taxes.
Actually, some do avoid paying taxes,
but nobody can escape death.
Are you ready for yours?

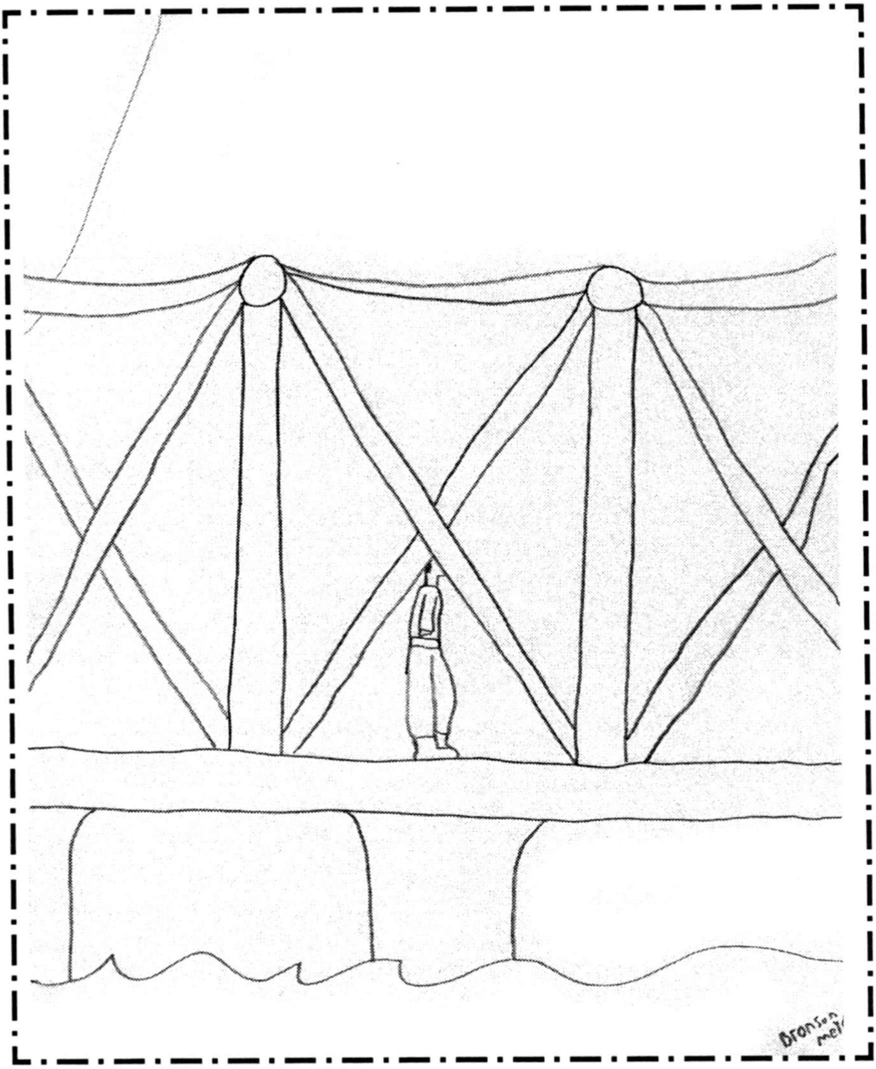
Bronson

Bridge by Bronson M.

CHAPTER SEVEN

A FRESH START

• • • • • • • • • • • • • • • •

The God who created us
holds our future in His hands.

• • • • • • • • • • • • • • • •

SISTER, SISTER

I can relate to the Biblical story of Mary and Martha (Luke chapter 10). Like these two sisters, my own sister and I are opposites.

When I was growing up, I shared a room with my sister, Miss Clean. We were like the odd couple. Cleaning to me meant shoving the moldy sandwiches under the bed. She, on the other hand, vacuumed the driveway, bleached the ceiling, and ironed her socks.

My sister likes to see how fast she can get housework done, while I like to do a little here and a little there over the course of a few years. Her house looks like the cover of a magazine. Mine looks like a landfill. Her floors are so clean you could eat off them. You can eat off my floors too . . . if you're a dog.

Cleanliness may be next to godliness, but perfectionistic cleanliness is next to annoying.

Martha was a conscientious, committed, and hard-working perfectionist. (I was like that when I first got married, before I stopped cleaning and cooking real meals.) Martha was a dynamo who got things done; and they were done right. I'm sure she enjoyed the praise and appreciation of all who knew her. She was one of those "type A" super-mom, wonder-woman personalities that I just have to hate because they are sooo perfect. You know the kind; they start washing the dishes before the family's finished eating, and they get up early to vacuum the hair from the bathroom floor before churning butter and threshing wheat to bake homemade bread. Martha was the type of woman who would never have left for church on Sunday morning with her house looking like it had been ransacked by a bunch of hoodlums named Guido, Vinnie, and Knuckles.

Martha's sister Mary was her opposite. She probably irritated and frustrated Martha. Mary was just too relaxed. When there was dirty laundry to beat on the river rocks and grain to grind, I'll bet Mary didn't stress over it. She probably didn't get excited when the dog tracked mud in on the new Berber carpet either. I'm guessing Mary didn't care if yesterday's lasagna was encrusted on the dishes, and I doubt that she concerned herself with cat hair accumulating so thick that it looked like a shag rug. Chances are that she didn't mind fingerprints on the glass patio doors. Well, okay, they didn't have carpeting, lasagna, or glass doors then; but you get my point. Mary just didn't have the same priorities her sister had, and she didn't do things the way Martha did. That made Martha resentful. She wanted things the way she wanted things! (Does that attitude remind you of anyone?) Martha thought her sister was not doing her share around the house. It upset her that Mary didn't care about important things, like getting supper on the table at exactly the right time, combing all the rug fringes in the same direction, never leaving dirty dishes in the sink for later, and having all the canned vegetables in alphabetical order on the pantry shelves.

If you've read the story of these two sisters, you know I've exaggerated it; but you also know which sister was more pleasing to Jesus. Yep, that would be Mary. Her desire was not to get things done or make things look good. In fact, her desire was not to "do" anything. Mary desired just to "be" with her Lord. And that's what He desired too. Jesus said, *"Martha, Martha, you are worried and upset about many things, but only one thing is needed. Mary has chosen what is better."* (Luke 10:42 & 43)

This story reminds me that I don't have to work to earn God's mercy and love. *"The Lord does not look at the things man looks at. Man looks at the outward appearance, but the Lord looks at the heart."* (1 Samuel 16:6-8)

Thank God He loves me no matter what my abilities (or disabilities) are. When I was younger and healthier, I was more of a human doing than a human being. I tried to be the perfect mom, getting up at 4:00 in the morning to do housework, and making my son's school lunches with fresh, home-baked bread. I helped every group that needed volunteers, and I was involved in almost every church project. Then I got sick. Because of debilitating fatigue, migraines, chronic muscle and joint pain, and recurring depression, I had to stop teaching Sunday School, tutoring at my son's school, leading scouting groups–in fact, I had to stop everything. Because of foot and leg pain, I had to spend a lot of time lying around. While I was doing nothing, I had plenty of time to feel guilty about it. I realized that—until that time—my self-esteem had hinged on what I could do. Suddenly unable to maintain a whirlwind pace of frenzied activity, I felt unworthy and unimportant.

Later, I learned that God doesn't have unrealistic expectations of me. He accepts and loves me even when I am unable to do anything. All He expects is for me to return the love He lavishes on me and to share it with others. I'm free from striving to do more and more. How comforting to relax in God's unconditional love! The psalmist wrote, "*I trust in God's unfailing love forever and ever.*" (Psalm 52:8) My attitude means more to God than what I do. Good works are temporary and won't be with me when I see Him face to face. Matthew chapter seven says many on judgment day will recall the multitude of good things they did in the name of Jesus, but He will declare "*I never knew you. Depart from me.*"

I don't want to be in that group, separated from the one I worked to serve, do you? I want to invest time and effort developing my relationship with God, because that is the one thing that will last forever and be of value when I meet Him.

I don't do many of the things I used to do. Thank God, I don't have to do anything to guarantee my entrance into heaven. There are many Christians who can do more than I can, but, like the woman in Mark 14:8, I do what I can; and that's all that God expects. I do it for Him out of love, not out of compulsion or fear of what others might think.

Life is not a series of projects to be carried out. It's a journey with the goal of traveling closer to God, knowing Him better, and allowing Him to perfect me for His kingdom.

When I ask God to lead me in His will, He brings me opportunities to serve Him. Others may not notice; but that doesn't matter. I'm not looking for their praise. God is the one I want to please and serve.

Who are you striving to please?

Mary by Michaela B.

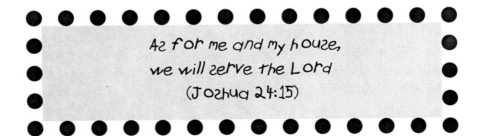

As for me and my house,
we will serve the Lord
(Joshua 24:15)

COMPUTERS, DYNAMITE, AND SLEDGE HAMMERS

Computers are wonderful machines. How did we ever manage without them? They save us a lot of time. They help us do things that would have been impossible thirty years ago. My computer has replaced my brain since my memory crashed.

I have a love/hate relationship with this modern marvel of technology. Most of the time, I think it's the greatest thing since sliced chocolate cake. However, when it malfunctions, I get frustrated and fantasize about throwing it off my roof, blowing it up with dynamite, or smashing it with a sledge hammer.

When this little machine wreaks havoc in my life, it brings everything to a screeching halt. I've spent the last two days trying to fix damage done by viruses. I've erased files, downloaded other files, and searched for strange things like worms, trojans, and spies. Sometimes computer problems can be solved. Other times, it's hopeless and the machine must be discarded and replaced.

But there's a wonderful little secret I've learned that can solve many computer problems, if they're not too serious. It's a quick, easy, remedy that even computer illiterate people can do. When the P.C. is running slow, not doing what I want it to do, or freezing up and refusing to work at all, I can often fix it in a second. I just press the "control," "alt," and "delete" keys. It's like magic! The malfunctioning machine shapes up. I get a new page, a fresh start, and a perfectly working machine. Problem solved. Life is good again.

Life can be compared to a computer. I sometimes want to take the sledge hammer approach when things aren't working right. I get frustrated and discouraged, and sometimes I freeze up, getting stuck in habits I can't free myself from. When things go haywire, I can get so messed up that I can't function. Yet, life can be good again. I may not have a control key, like my computer, but Jesus is the key that can wipe out my past and provide a fresh start. He'll reboot me.

Handing over the keyboard of my life to Jesus and letting Him control my CPU won't get me a new PC, but He'll wipe out the hard drive of my past and give me a clean slate and a fresh start. A new computer is nice, but a new life is even better.

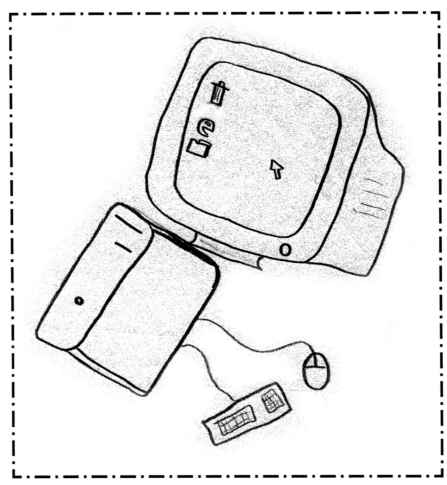

Computer by Bronson M.

As viruses infect computers,
sin infects our souls,
but God can salvage us.

DATE TO REMEMBER

My birthday is close to Christmas, so people often forget about it. I've considered celebrating my half birthday instead, in the middle of summer. Or I could celebrate monthly birthdays like kids often do. Just the other day, my grandson proudly announced, "I'm six and a half years old! But most people celebrate only one birthday each year. In case you're interested, mine is January 2.

I have a friend who often doesn't receive birthday gifts from me. I miss her special day nearly every year. She's so humble that she never reminds me, and she loves me in spite of my forgetfulness. She's unselfish and noble. I admire her, but I'm not at all like her. That's why I'm telling you now, in advance, to mark my birthday on your calendar. It's *January 2*. Write it in big, red letters so it's easy to read. And highlight it with a yellow marker so you can't miss it. Also, make a note to purchase a lavish gift in honor of the occasion. I considered registering at some expensive stores, but I decided that would be tacky.

If you think you might not remember this special day (*January 2*), I could send you a daily email to let you know the exact number of shopping days left till *January 2*.

Even if you do forget the date, (Did I mention it's *January 2*?) that's okay. I don't mind receiving gifts late. In fact, I rarely celebrate my birthday only on *January 2*. I prefer to party the entire week. I like to party, and I'm happy to make it through another year; so why not celebrate all month long?

I used to think I had no talents; but I've discovered that I really do. My talents are partying, making merry, having fun, and receiving nice gifts each year on *January 2*. These talents are very important to society. Generous people like *you* need people like *me* in their lives so they have someone to give all those extravagant gifts to (on *January 2*, especially).

I love getting gifts, even if they're from strangers or enemies. Hey, if they're willing to give, I'm willing to receive! That's why I'm surprised there are folks in this world who have been offered the best gift of all time, but they won't accept it. Doesn't make much sense, does it? I hope you are not one of those people.

You know the gift I'm referring to. It's the greatest gift God had to give. Who else would sacrifice His son for someone else? God sent His son to suffer and die for our sinfulness. Jesus endured torture so that you and I could someday live with Him in heaven. How much more generous could a giver be? With His son's blood, God paid for our tickets to heaven. Isn't it sad that so many refuse that gift?

I was kidding about wanting you to remember my birthday, but I do hope you'll remember the most important day in history, when Jesus died for you.

In the second chapter of Acts, Peter told the people, *"Repent and be baptized for the forgiveness of your sins; and you will receive the gift of the Holy Spirit."*

I don't want you to give me birthday gifts; but God wants to give you the gift of salvation, which Jesus made possible. Will you receive it with gratitude?

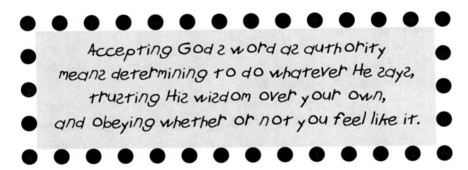

Accepting God's word as authority
means determining to do whatever He says,
trusting His wisdom over your own,
and obeying whether or not you feel like it.

Gift by Kaitlyn Marie S.

WHAT ARE YOU WEARING?

This morning I put moisturizer on to hide my wrinkles, makeup to cover my age spots, and mascara to make my lashes look longer. I thought about all the effort I put into disguising the real me. I color my gray hair, pluck my chin hairs, and buy clothes that will (hopefully) make me look thinner. Heaven forbid if someone should see what I really look like!

And it's not just my outside appearance I try to hide. I wonder how often people see me for who I really am. Do they see only what I want them to see? When I lose my cool, my real attitudes come spewing out, and it's usually not the side of me that I like to show people.

We all pretend at times to be something we're not. It's natural to hide our faults so people will like us. Just like the characters at Disney World, we wear masks to disguise our real selves and please those around us. We may be able to fool some of the people some of the time, but we can't fool God. He sees through our disguises into our hearts.

Jesus told the Pharisees (in Matthew 23:27) *"You are like whitewashed tombs, which look beautiful on the outside but on the inside are full of dead men's bones and everything unclean. On the outside you appear to people as righteous, but on the inside you are full of hypocrisy and wickedness."*

God knows our thoughts and motives (Psalm 139). The prophet Isaiah wrote (in Isaiah 64) that all the good deeds we do to cover up our sinful side and all of our best efforts to look good appear no better than filthy rags to God. Sound discouraging?

Here's the GOOD news: Even though God knows who we really are, He loves us in spite of our failures and weaknesses. He wants to clothe us in "garments of salvation" and cover us with "robes of righteousness." (Isaiah 61:10)

Galatians 3:27 says that when you're baptized, you "clothe" yourself with Christ. You don't need a mask or a costume to disguise your real self. If you want something to cover up your bad side or if you need someone to hide behind, it can be Jesus. You can be covered by God's grace, salvation, and righteousness. And, unlike worldly clothes, these garments last for eternity. When you put these on, they don't just cover your faults and disguise you— they make you a whole new person (2 Corinthians 5:17). What a relief! Instead of trying to hide the real you, let God change you from the inside out into something better. He can give you a new heart (Ezekiel 26:36) with new desires. He'll create a new spirit within you. Then you won't have to worry about pretending, hiding, or covering up.

With all your failures and faults, you may feel like an ugly caterpillar right now; but with God's power, you can be transformed into a new creation, like a beautiful butterfly!

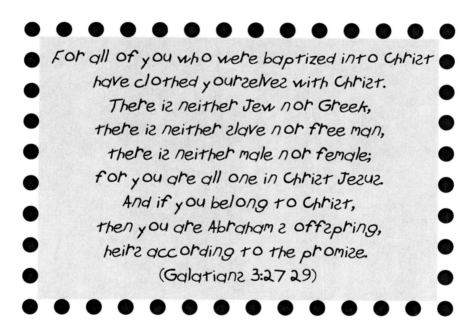

For all of you who were baptized into Christ
have clothed yourselves with Christ.
There is neither Jew nor Greek,
there is neither slave nor free man,
there is neither male nor female;
for you are all one in Christ Jesus.
And if you belong to Christ,
then you are Abraham's offspring,
heirs according to the promise.
(Galatians 3:27 29)

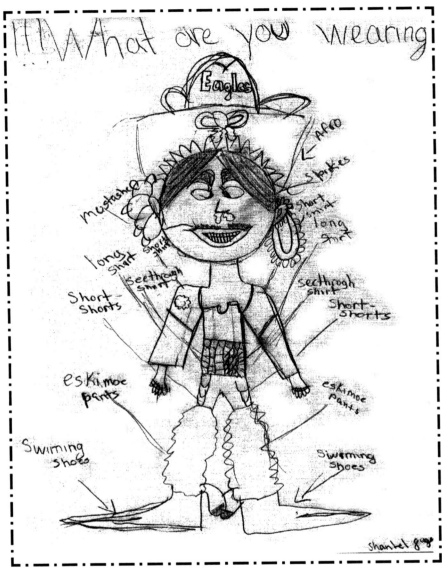

What are you wearing? by Shantel S.

WHAT NOW?

I know a lot of people who ask, "How can we know where we stand with God?" If we repent, are we righteous in His sight? If we ask Jesus to be part of our life or take up residence in our heart, can we be confident of our salvation?

The Bible does talk about these things—and much more. To discover the whole truth about anything God wants us to know, I've found that we need to read all the Scripture passages on that subject. We can get the entire picture if we put all verses on a topic together.

Below are a few of many New Testament scriptures that refer to how we can know for certain that Jesus has paid the debt we owed for sin. Let's let God's word itself answer the question, "How do I know I'm saved?"

2 Thessalonians 2:10 says those who love the truth will be saved.

Romans 10:9 says those who confess Jesus before men will be saved.

Mark 16:16 says those who believe and are baptized shall be saved.

Acts 2:21 says everyone who calls on the name of the Lord will be saved.

Acts 2:36-38 says repent and be baptized for forgiveness of your sins. (See also 2 Corinthians 7)

Acts 16:30-32 says believe in the Lord Jesus and you will be saved.

Acts 22:16 says be baptized to wash away your sins, calling on His name.

1 Peter 3:21 says baptism now saves you.

Wait a minute! Each of these verses says something different about what leads to salvation. Which is right? Do they contradict each other? Which ones should I obey?

They are *all* directives from God. His word can't contradict itself. If we put all these instructions together, the full scope of what God is saying will be clearer. From His own Word, then, what can we conclude about redemption?

One must first *love the truth*. (In order to do that, we must read God's Word to know what it says, believe that it came from God, and determine to live by it.)

In addition, we must *believe* in God, His Son, and His Word, and we must have *faith*. (Faith is more than mere head belief. It involves trusting God enough to respond to His desires as He has directed. This type of "acting faith" or trust will lead us to benefit from the saving work that Jesus accomplished by shedding His blood.)

When we have learned what God's Word says, we will see that we have all fallen short of what God intended for us. If we love Him, we will believe and love His word. We will believe in His son Jesus and what He did for us. All this will naturally cause us to *repent* of our sins and turn from our past way of life.

According to the scriptures, in addition to repenting, we also need to *confess* Jesus (express trust in the sacrifice and resurrection of Jesus) and *call upon the Name of the* LORD as we are *baptized* to "wash away our sins."

Do these verses mean that by our actions we earn our salvation? No way! Our salvation was earned by the actions of Jesus. None of God's commands involve us working our own way to heaven. By obeying God's directives, we are simply receiving (at the time and in the manner that He dictates) the salvation that Jesus paid for and made available to us.

For instance, the verse of scripture that says "baptism now washes away your sins" (Acts 22:16) is speaking not of *how* we are saved, but when and where we receive the gift of salvation that was bought by the blood of Jesus. His blood is what saves us, but we decide if and when we will accept it. We re-enact His death and burial by going down into the water, and we re-enact His resurrection when we come back up out of the water.

Who should decide the terms on which we come to God? We can't. God has determined how we receive His gift of salvation. He has that right, since He sacrificed his own son to make salvation possible. He alone can tell us how He wants us to enter through the wall that our sin created, which has kept us from fellowship with Him.

Though none of these steps save us, they are commands from God. Are any of them so difficult that we cannot obey them?

What will keep you from accepting the gift of salvation that Jesus died to give you?

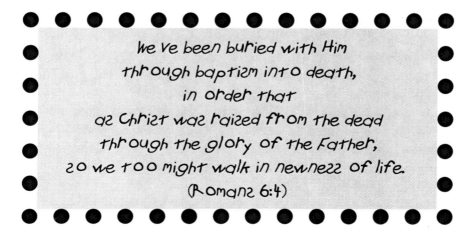

We've been buried with Him
through baptism into death,
in order that
as Christ was raised from the dead
through the glory of the Father,
so we too might walk in newness of life.
(Romans 6:4)

GIFT ON THE PORCH

Christmas with my grandson is fun because he can read his name now. His face lights up when he recognizes the letters C-O-B-I on a package. No matter what our age, don't we all like to receive presents? YOU have reason to be excited, because the greatest gift of all time has *your* name on it. Unfortunately, many people miss out on this valuable gift, because they don't accept it.

Imagine that I carefully chose a wonderful present for you and wrapped it in beautiful paper tied with a huge, colorful bow. Let's say I delivered this gift to your home and left it on your front porch. You, however, were inside the house unaware that something wonderful awaited outside the door. The gift was bought with you in mind and delivered right to your door; but as far as you were concerned, you did not have any gift from me. Why? Because you had not opened your door, taken the gift into your house, and opened it. By doing these things, you would be accepting my gift. Only after you receive a gift does it really belong to you. Now, imagine that God prepared a wonderful gift for you. The gift is salvation, made possible through Jesus. Even though God intends it for everyone and offers it to all the world, salvation belongs only to those who accept it.

Some believe that if you make an effort to accept the gift, that detracts from the giver. On the contrary, you honor the giver when you graciously accept what he offers. Your acceptance of a present doesn't mean you're responsible for providing it. If not for the giver, you couldn't receive the gift; so you can't take credit for it. Salvation comes from God, not from your efforts. Yet, you must accept His gift in order to own it for yourself.

When a large crowd of Jews asked Peter on Pentecost how they could receive the gift of salvation, this was what he told them, *"Repent and be baptized in the name of Jesus Christ for the remission of sins, and you shall receive the gift of the Holy Spirit."* (Acts 2:38)

The passage goes on to say that those who believed what Peter said, and were baptized, were then added to the church (verse 41).

I hope you won't leave God's soul-saving gift on the porch of your life. Instead, I would encourage you to open your heart's door, reach out to God, and actively accept the gift of salvation, according to His instructions.

"The wages of sin is death, but the gift of God is eternal life through Jesus Christ." (Romans 6:23) *"Thanks be to God for His indescribable gift!"* (2 Corinthians 9:15)

Gift on the Porch by Rachel S.

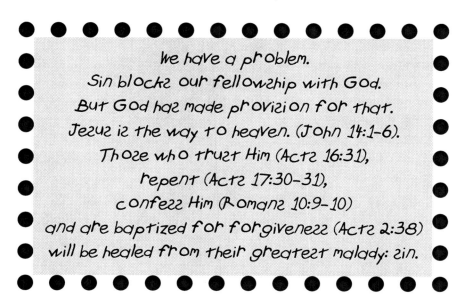

We have a problem.
Sin blocks our fellowship with God.
But God has made provision for that.
Jesus is the way to heaven. (John 14:1-6).
Those who trust Him (Acts 16:31),
repent (Acts 17:30-31),
confess Him (Romans 10:9-10)
and are baptized for forgiveness (Acts 2:38)
will be healed from their greatest malady: sin.

THREE B'S

Once I had realized I was in the same boat as all other humans in the world, and I needed a savior, I decided to turn away from my own ways and turn toward God. Then, I found that there were three things I needed to remember, in order for everything else in life to fall into place. All of these three begin with "B."

They are baptism, belong, and Bible.

When I was baptized, I re-enacted the death, burial, and resurrection of Jesus. *"Therefore we have been buried with Him through baptism into death, in order that as Christ was raised from the dead through the glory of the Father, so we too might walk in newness of life."* (Romans 6:4) Allowing myself to be baptized proved that I wanted to die to my old way of life and let God give me a new life. The Bible says sins are washed away in the waters of baptism (Acts 22:16), so I had a clean, fresh start.

The second important "B" word is belong. When God added me to His family, I become part of the Body of Christ. (2 Corinthians 12:27) I was where I belonged. I then needed to get to know other Christians and spend time with them. They helped me learn how to live my new life.

The third "B" word to remember is Bible. Jesus said that in order to grow closer to God and maintain a relationship with Him, we need to "abide" in His word. Abide means to be in it constantly. Of course, we can't carry a Bible wherever we go; but we can read it daily and meditate on what we've learned from it. Then we'll be able to put into practice the lessons God's Word has taught us.

The three important "B" words will get our lives on track and help to keep them there.

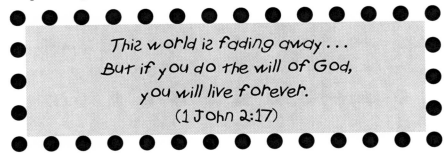

This world is fading away . . .
But if you do the will of God,
you will live forever.
(1 John 2:17)

LORD, I AM GRATEFUL

God, how can I say thanks for all you've done for me?
For standing beside me on the lonely road of fear,
For lifting me out of the dry valley of despair,
For holding me close during the thundering storms of doubt,
Lord, I'm grateful.
For walking before me through the dark forest of trepidation,
For carrying me over the river of worry,
For bathing me in the fountain of peace,
Lord, I am grateful.
For clothing me with the robe of your forgiveness,
For covering me with the veil of your mercy,
For pouring over me the perfume of hope,
Lord, I am grateful.

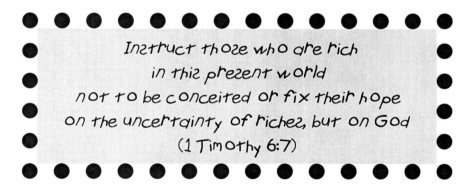

Instruct those who are rich
in this present world
not to be conceited or fix their hope
on the uncertainty of riches, but on God
(1 Timothy 6:7)

Boy and Girl by Elizabeth S.

CHAPTER EIGHT

LOOKING FORWARD

Anything that brings me closer to God is a good thing.

LIMBURGER ATTITUDE

I don't like morning—it starts too early in the day. Yesterday morning was worse than most and started out bad from the get go. I always know it's going to be a lousy day when it begins with getting out of bed. I've had bronchitis for over a week, and to make matters worse, I awoke with a migraine the size of Hoboken, New Jersey. I was crabbier than a seaside restaurant.

I'd had surgery on my hand and was taking pain medication that made me lethargic, so I just wanted to veg out, watching *Gilligan's Island* reruns and old movies. But right in the middle of "It's a Wonderful Life," my TV died. (Merry Christmas, Bedford Falls!) I don't know what went wrong with it, but it may have had something to do with the flames shooting out the back like fourth of July fireworks.

Do you know how boring and frustrating it is to be cranky, tired, and sick but not have a TV for distraction? I had to put up with my own company. That's as much fun as spending the day in a phone booth with a Pitt Bull that has PMS.

I decided to make Christmas cookies, but that endeavor did not go well. The first bowl of dough was runnier than my nose. The second batch was as sticky as used gum on a hot sidewalk, and I burned the third batch blacker than a grease monkey's finger nails. No wonder I hate to cook. After three flops, I gave up and vowed never to touch an oven mitt again. I think I'll become a commercial cook, cooking only what can be heated in the microwave during TV commercials.

I grabbed the pitcher of juice and bumped it on the counter. The bottom exploded like an overcooked Johnsonville brat. A geyser of juice and shattered glass sprayed the cupboards and floor. After cleaning that up, I went into the den and slid across the room on a pile of dog vomit, smearing it all over the rug. Another mess to clean up.

The last straw was when I went to the drug store for antibiotics. When the pharmacist told me it would cost $60 for three days' worth, I got madder than a constipated rattlesnake. And like a rattlesnake, I wanted to bite somebody. I didn't have that much money on me, so I had to leave without the pills.

When I got back home, I stomped around complaining about everything that annoyed me. Being crankier than a giraffe with strep throat, I couldn't think of a single thing that didn't bug me.

Coincidentally, while listening to the radio, I heard a country song entitled, "I hate everything." My sentiments exactly!

Then I recalled a funny story about a kid pulling a prank on his grandpa. While the old man slept, his grandson wiped Limburger cheese on his mustache. When grandpa woke up, he complained that the room smelled bad. When he walked into a different room, that one smelled the same way. Finally, he went outside to get away from the odor, but it followed him. Grandpa exclaimed, "The whole world stinks!"

Yesterday, even without Limburger cheese on my face, I felt like the whole world stunk.

Of course, I know that this kind of thinking results from focusing on the negative and not seeing the positive. When I do that, I say things like "always," "never," or "everybody." For instance, "EVERYBODY else has a better life than I do." Or "Things NEVER work out for me." And "Why do bad things ALWAYS happen to me?" I know very well that everybody doesn't have a better life. Bad things don't always happen to only me; but yesterday, it sure did seem that way.

When I have a "Limburger attitude," and feel like the whole world smells bad, I need to challenge my false self talk. To adjust my "stinkin' thinkin'," I remember what the apostle Paul endured. He had a lot more "bad luck" than any of us could experience in a life time; and if anyone had a right to complain, Paul did. Yet, while in prison, he wrote, "*Rejoice in the Lord always . . .*" (Philippians 4:4) How in the world can a person be happy when everything's going wrong?

Reading some of Paul's other letters helps to shed some light on his perspective. In his second letter to the Corinthian church (chapter 11) he wrote, "*Five times I received from the Jews forty lashes minus one. Three times I was beaten with rods; once I was stoned; three times I was shipwrecked; I spent a night and a day in the open sea; I have been constantly on the move. I have been in danger from rivers; in danger from bandits; in danger from my own countrymen; in danger from Gentiles; in danger in the city; in danger in the country; in danger at sea; and in danger from false brothers. I have labored and toiled and have often gone without sleep; I have known hunger and thirst and have often gone without food; I have been cold and naked. Besides everything else, I face daily the pressure of my concern for all the churches.*"

Paul had a lot on his shoulders. Why was it not crushing his spirit? He wrote in 2 Corinthians 4, "*We are hard pressed on every side, but not crushed; perplexed, but not in despair; persecuted, but not abandoned; struck down, but not destroyed.*" The phrase there that jumps out at me is "not abandoned." Paul knew that he was not alone, and he could depend upon God staying with him, no matter what happened. That's the key to contentment.

Paul could not control his circumstances, and neither can we. However, like Paul, we can control our attitudes. Reversing a Limburger attitude requires developing an attitude of gratitude. When I feel that everything is bad and the world stinks, I need to stop and make a conscious effort to focus on the positive. I think of the good things for which I can be thankful. If nothing else, I can be thankful that I woke up this morning. (Well, maybe there are some days when that doesn't SEEM like such a positive thing.)

There's at least one thing for which we can all be grateful: God cares for us and is willing to walk with us through difficulties. That in itself is reason to rejoice. I heard someone say, "Nothing can happen to me today that God and I together can't handle." That's good to remember.

When I count my blessings, I feel bad about the way I whine and feel sorry for myself. I have a lot more than many others do. I have much to be thankful for and nothing to complain about.

Negative self talk can make me feel like the whole world stinks, but positive thinking is just as powerful. Practicing thankfulness often turns my outlook around. A Limburger attitude can become an attitude of gratitude.

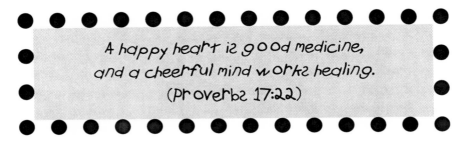

A happy heart is good medicine,
and a cheerful mind works healing.
(Proverbs 17:22)

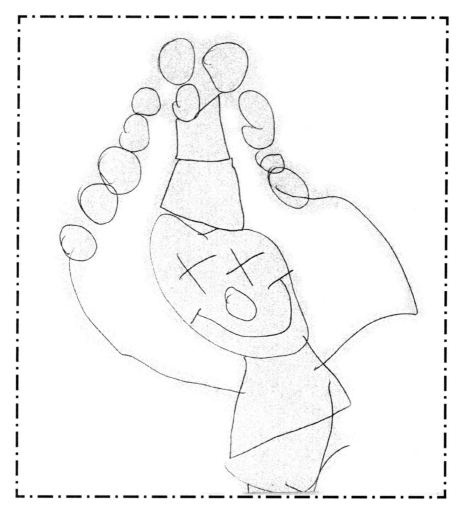

Happy Clown by Meghan J.

MR. POTATO HEART

I heard a story of a man who put three pots on the stove to boil. He put a potato into one pot. In another he placed an egg, and into the third pot he dropped some coffee beans.

In half an hour, the man pulled all three out of the water. The potato had been hard, but the adversity of boiling water weakened it and made it soft. The egg, which had gone into the water fragile, came out hardened. The boiling water brought out the best of the coffee beans.

Which best represents your heart? When tough times bubble up in your life like boiling water, how do you respond? Do pain and heat sap your strength and make you wilt? After divorce, death, or financial ruin does your soft heart turn hard and bitter? Or are you like the coffee bean, which doesn't reach its peak unless it's heated to two-hundred and twelve degrees?

I don't want a heart like a potato or an egg. I'm aspiring to be a coffee bean. How about you?

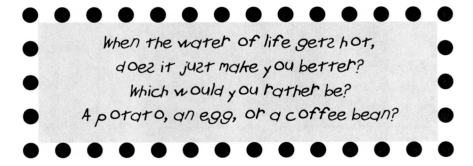

When the water of life gets hot,
does it just make you better?
Which would you rather be?
A potato, an egg, or a coffee bean?

Mr. Potato Head by Latosha S.

LITTLE ACTS OF LOVE

As I loaded the lunch dishes into the dishwasher, I sang along with the radio. My grandson looked up from the picture he was coloring and said, "Grandma, there's one thing about you that I don't like." Anticipating what he was going to say, I asked, "What? That I sing all the time?"

"No," he answered, "It's not how much you sing, it's how *bad* you sing." Once again, I was reminded that God did not bless me with a good singing voice.

I envy wonderful singers who entertain millions of adoring fans packed into crowded stadiums. My singing can't even please one six year old. I've always envied people who could speak eloquently. I have trouble completing a sentence that can be understood by a preschooler.

I may not possess the talents I would have preferred to be born with, but I still have the ability to change the world . . . and so do you!

It doesn't require wealth, talent, or a huge investment of time. Right now, you (yes you), with your current limitations and abilities, have tremendous power to impact others.

Don't believe me? Have you ever had a day in which everything you touched went wrong? When you were at the end of your rope, did someone speak a kind word or help you out? Do you remember how it warmed your heart and perked up your spirit? Small, loving acts make a profound difference. Everyone longs to feel noticed and appreciated. That's why it means so much when someone surprises us with a simple act of caring. It assures us that we matter.

Discouraged people are everywhere. They need you. Don't overlook opportunities to make a difference in someone's life. A smile, a note, or a phone call won't take much effort, but they can make someone's day. Not only will your kindness be appreciated by the recipient and rewarded by God, but it will enrich your own life too.

Many folks say, "I'm just one person. I can't make a difference." If you've ever been on the receiving end of a hug just when it's needed, you know one person's concern is powerful. Do you compare your contribution to a tiny drop of water in the huge ocean? Mother Theresa's view was that the ocean would be less without that one drop.

There could be no mountains, if not for the tiny grains of sand from which the mountains are made. Little things pack a big punch. Encouragement takes only a moment to give but it delivers an important message of love and concern to the recipient, and it could last a lifetime. Your empathy and time can lessen someone's load and make their life journey easier.

We may not speak like Billy Graham or sing like Frank Sinatra, but we each have our own unique talents that God wants us to use. Have you considered that you may be exactly what someone is praying for? Open your heart. Show you care. Share a little love.

Acts of love by Shantel S.

Marsha Jordan

Be kind to one another, tenderhearted.
(Ephesians 4:31)

There's some discouraged brother
Who is needing you today
To smile or to talk with him
Or kneel with him to pray.

Some weary, burdened sister
Has longed to hear you say,
"I'll be your friend, I'll hold your hand.
I'll help you on your way."

The smallest act of kindness,
A word of cheer you've spoken
Can lift a heavy burden
And heal a heart that's broken.

Don't overlook a chance to help
Discouraged folks to see
That God's Word is calling,
"If you're weary, come to me."

As God looks down from heaven
And sees you share His love,
He'll reward your earnest effort
And send blessings from above.

Use the talents that He gave you
Whether great or small.
Send a message to the world
Of how He loves us all.

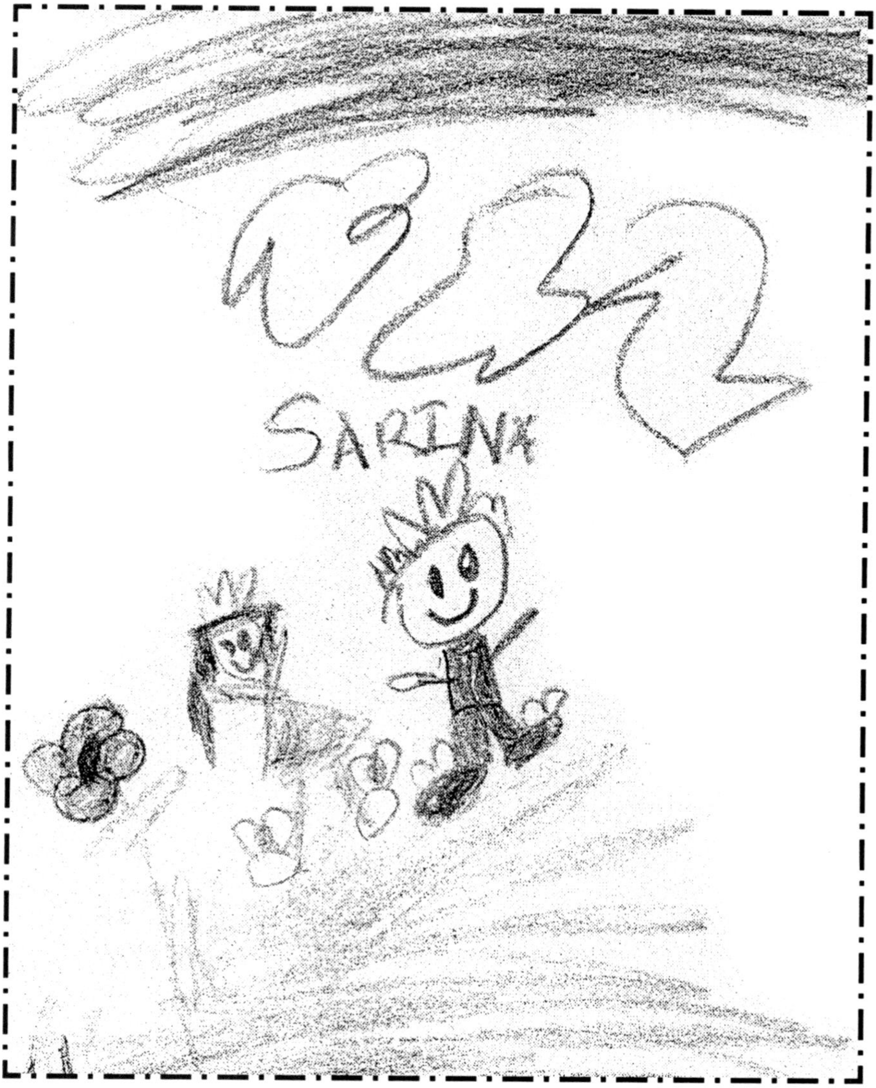
SARINA

Boy and girl by Sarina S.

You can share some love with sick children who need cheer.
Send a card and a smile. Join the Hugs and Hope Club
(www.hugsandhope.org)
and make a difference for kids, one smile at a time.

Mailbox by Caleb L

HELP! I'VE BECOME MY MOTHER

I swore it would never happen, but it did. I noticed it one sweltering August afternoon in 2001. I opened my mouth and . . . out came my mother's voice! I was saying all the things I'd long ago sworn never to repeat. *I had become my mother!*

I really can't be blamed, though. Can I help it that I've lived long enough to acquire more wisdom than the average woman? And along with all that wisdom has come an irresistible urge to share it—with everyone—all the time!

I'm not surprised that I'm the wisest woman I know. Just think about it. I've experienced things that today's kids know about only through textbooks. I watched the Beatles' first performance on The Ed Sullivan Show. I owned one of the first hoola hoops (though I don't recall ever mastering the use of it). It even fit around my waist back then. I learned to read with Dick and Jane, and I nearly flunked third grade when "new math" was introduced. I watched Bonanza before it became reruns. I experienced the thrill of replacing our black and white television with color and the anxiety of seeing a brother leave for Viet Nam. I lived through the turmoil of the civil rights movement and witnessed the assassination of John Kennedy on television. I saw hippies putting flowers in their hair and protesting the war, females burning their bras for women's liberation, and black children entering white schools to end segregation. I'm a veritable walking encyclopedia and a living history book, for Pete's sake. Why SHOULDN'T everyone listen to me? My brain is a storehouse of vast knowledge. Unfortunately, I'm the only one who realizes this, except for my dog, King Louie, who idolizes me.

Do you know how difficult it is to bite my tongue when I see so many unfortunate souls making the same mistakes I've made? The impulse to teach others what I've had to learn firsthand is as hard to resist as a super fudge chocolate swirl ice cream sundae with brownie bits and extra hot fudge.

No wonder I was voted Know-it-all of the year by Buttinskies Anonymous. But, alas, people don't seem as eager to learn as I am eager to teach them. In fact, have you noticed how people are not receptive at all to unsolicited advice?

After thousands of well-intentioned attempts to spread my wisdom to the masses, it occurred to me that when someone shares their problems, they're not asking for my advice. They need someone to listen as they vent and to acknowledge their pain, not enumerate a detailed list of solutions. People don't care how much you know. They want to know how much you care.

So, here is a bit of advice from one of the world's wisest women: "*Rejoice with those who rejoice, and weep with those who weep.*" Actually, I can't take credit for that bit of wisdom. It comes from the Bible (Romans 12: 15, NKJV); and it reminds me to just "be there" for others, rather than trying to solve their problems. A warm touch means more to a hurting person than a list of recommendations. My friends don't need a mother, they need a friend who listens while they talk, holds their hand when they're afraid, and hugs them when they cry.

Do you know someone who could use a friend and a hug today?

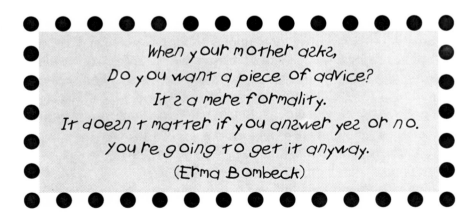

When your mother asks,
Do you want a piece of advice?
It's a mere formality.
It doesn't matter if you answer yes or no.
You're going to get it anyway.
(Erma Bombeck)

WISDOM

Because I love to share my knowledge with the world, I have packed into one paragraph, a condensed version of all the wisdom I've gleaned from common cliches. Here is my (not necessarily good) advice:

If you can't say something nice, quit while you're ahead because an ounce of prevention is good for the gander and gathers no moss. When in doubt, eat lots of chocolate and let sleeping dogs take time to smell all your eggs in one basket. Crime doesn't pay for your bridges behind you. Practice makes a rolling stone look a gift horse in the mouth and spoil the soup. Too many cooks spare the rod and go to bed with the early bird. Look before you leap because money is the root of death and taxes.

Someone, somewhere, revised some other familiar phrases from the fifties and sixties to modernize them for the zeros. I don't know who gets credit for writing these, but they're words to live by:

Children should be seen and not costing me money. When push comes to shove, their mom is on the phone. People who live in glass houses can't watch TV in their underwear. If you can't say something nice, you must be with your in-laws. Where there's smoke, my husband's been cooking. You can fool some of the people some of the time, but you can't make a man change a toilet paper roll. A pound of chocolate is worth its weight in gold. Time flies when you're checking your email. Nothing is certain except that your computer will crash when you haven't saved any files.

And, here's my favorite bit of wisdom: Better to have loved and lost than to never have tasted chocolate.

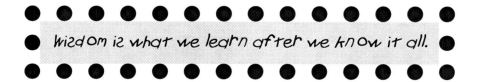

Wisdom is what we learn after we know it all.

HE DID WHAT HE COULD

John the Baptist didn't have any great talents. He didn't perform mystifying miracles (not even a simple card trick). He wasn't a handsome crooner with a voice like Perry Como's. He didn't have degrees or diplomas. He didn't have an impressive gift of speaking like Billy Graham. He wasn't popular, since he offended people by calling them such names as vipers and white washed tombs. John was not a snappy dresser. He made his clothes from camel's hair. He was just a common man, a scruffy sort of guy with strange eating habits (locusts). He didn't have a job. He just wandered around talking to folks. He wasn't better, smarter, richer or any other "er." He was just a guy who told people about what he knew: *"One mightier than I is coming."* (Matthew 3:11) Do you ever wish you had a great talent to use for God and mankind? If you were a gifted surgeon, you could save lives. If you had a beautiful voice, you could sing about God's love around the world. If you were a good speaker, you could preach to millions.

Most of us, like John the Baptist, are pretty ordinary. Yet Jesus said of John *"Among those that are born of women there is not a greater prophet than John the Baptist."* Wow, an ordinary guy (sort of strange, actually) was a great prophet. John did the best he could with the talents he had and it was enough. In fact, it was great. *"John did no miracle: but all things that John spoke of were true. And many believed on him there."* (John 10:41-42). John prepared the way for the Lord by telling the truth and leading people to Jesus.

I believe it was Mother Theresa who said, "There are no great deeds, only small deeds done with great love." Like John, we ordinary people can do whatever God has enabled us to do; and when we do it in love for Him, we can give Him no greater gift.

Man exists for God, not God for man.

MAGNIFYING MIRROR

I recently bought a magnifying mirror . . . a big, lighted magnifying mirror that makes it impossible for me to ignore all my face's imperfections. The unreasonable clerk who sold me the mirror wouldn't let me return it. She said not liking what I saw in it was not reason enough to get my money back.

Mirrors like this one should be illegal. It enlarges objects seven times their natural size. The thing is a health hazard. When I looked into it, I screamed in horror, then hyperventilated, passed out, and hit my head on the bathroom sink. I needed CPR to be resuscitated, and I think some of my brains might have been flushed down the toilet. I'm not sure I'll ever recover from discovering that my cheeks have pleats. (gasp!) The whole nasty experience plunged me into a state of third-degree, age-related depression.

All this time, I've been living in that lovely la-la-land of denial. I had fooled myself into believing that I still looked twenty-nine. Mother Nature played a cruel joke on me. Time to wake up and smell the extra-strength age spot remover. Reality hit me right between my puffy, sagging eyelids. Ouch! That smarts.

My laugh lines are no laughing matter, now that they're buried deep within my saggy cheeks. The only advantage is that I can finally say I have cleavage, even if it IS on my face. The black bags under my eyes are bigger than my feet. They're helping to save the forests, though. I carry groceries in them, rather than using the paper sacks at the grocery store.

I look like a puckered pile of flab and wrinkles with whiskers. When my husband calls me "pet," it's because my drooping jowls make me look like Cousin Delmont's old coon dog Otis, and my flabby neck jiggles like a Tom turkey's. My cheeks sag lower each day, like melting blobs of raspberry ripple ice cream. I'm afraid I'll awake some morning to discover that my face has slid down around my waist.

The dermatologist made my day when he called the dark patches on my cheeks "old age barnacles." I must look like a sunken ship. I asked him if plaster of paris might help, but instead he suggested that I have my face "resurfaced." So now I'm a well-traveled, worn out road? I must admit that my face does sort of look like a truck ran over it.

Wrinkles aren't the only revolting development that's got me down. It's bad enough that I've turned into grandma Moses, but I'm looking a lot like Grandpa Walton too. I've sprouted a beard and mustache, and my whole face is lower than it used to be. Yesterday, my husband called me "floppy cheeks," and I don't think he meant it as a term of endearment. I no longer count gravity among my friends. It's pulling everything southward, and parts that once were perky are now in danger of being stepped on and often get road rash from dragging on the pavement.

I've placed my youth on the endangered species list. It's evaporating faster than spit on a hot griddle. Instead of aging like a fine wine, I'm afraid I'm more like moldy cheese or curdled 2% milk. As my six-year-old grandson says, "I'm not happy about this."

You can understand why I appreciate the Bible verse in Proverbs 11, which says, "*A kind hearted woman will gain respect.*" I'm relieved, because I know I can't get by on my good looks. I hope people find my heart more pleasing to behold than the rest of me. I don't even know Grace, and I don't want to grow old with her, but I've found at least two things for which old timers can be thankful:

1) For those who love and obey Him, God does not examine faults with a magnifying glass. If He did, it would be a sight even more grotesque than the one staring back at me from my mirror. Instead, God is willing to remove each soul's blemishes and forget them forever. "*As far as the east is from the west, so far has He removed our transgressions from us.*" (Psalm 103:12)

2) Secondly, nobody is ever too old to be used by God. No matter what my age, or how many thousands of wrinkles and gray hairs I have, there is always something good I can do. God has plans for each of us. Jeremiah 29:11 says: "*I know the plans I have for you, 'declares the Lord, . . . to give you hope and a future.'*" We always have a place in God's scheme of things, even if one foot is in the rest home. We can't outgrow our usefulness and no one's ever too old to have hopes and dreams or to accomplish some pretty nifty things with God's help. I heard of one hip grandma who rode a

motorcycle on her ninetieth birthday. That sure beats staring at the wall from a rocking chair in a puddle of drool.

God doesn't just use young and beautiful people. In fact, I would guess that He can probably more often use older folks who have gained experience and learned the lessons that come only from making mistakes. How cool is it that He can work through anyone, wrinkles, age spots, and all? He'll use anybody, as long as they meet two requirements: A: they are willing, and B: they're still breathing.

That includes you. So open those wrinkled, baggy eyelids of yours and take a gander at the world around you. Forget your age. You will always be younger than someone somewhere. If you look, you'll see loads of things you can do. Get your pruney face and your varicose veins out there and get busy!

And by the way, if you have a magnifying mirror, toss it into the dumpster or give it to a young person. We have better things than wrinkles to focus on.

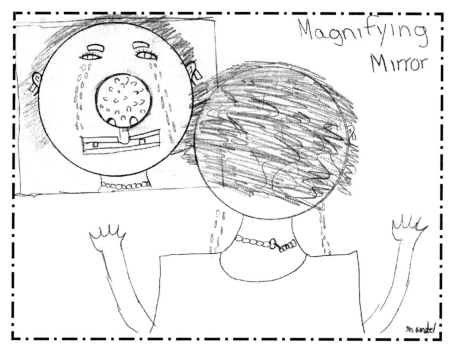

Magnifying mirror by Shantel S.

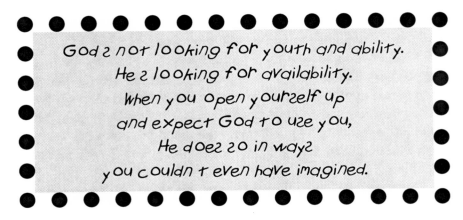

God's not looking for youth and ability.
He's looking for availability.
When you open yourself up
and expect God to use you,
He does so in ways
you couldn't even have imagined.

WHICH WAY TO GO?

Perseverance . . . Don't you hate it? You're tired, frustrated, and confused; but you have to hang in there anyway and keep plodding along. Sometimes, in fact a lot of the time, life seems too hard. But instead of fizzling *out*, caving *in*, lying *down*, and giving *up*, choose a different direction.

Rise *up* (as if on eagles' wings—Isaiah 40:3), fight to hang *in* there (1 Timothy 6:12), Press *on* (to the goal—Philippians 3:14), *over*come (1 John 4:4), and you will reap rewards (Galatians 6:9).

Do you think you just can't go on anymore? Read Philippians 4:13 and think again: *"I can do all things through Christ who strengthens me."*

Car by Josh P.

NOBODY APPRECIATES ME!

Have you ever felt forgotten, neglected, unappreciated, or unloved? Haven't we all?

Joseph, a prophet of God, was mistreated by his jealous brothers and just about everybody else he encountered. His brothers sold him as a slave and told their dad he'd been killed by a wild animal. With relatives like that, who needs enemies? But that was only the beginning of Joseph's trials.

He worked as a slave for a powerful man whose conniving wife tried repeatedly to seduce him. Though he refused her advances, she didn't give up. One day when she and Joseph were alone in the house, she pulled off his robe and he escaped in his underwear! The woman was so angry, she lied to her husband, saying Joseph had raped her. This, of course, did not go over well with Joseph's master. He threw Joseph into prison with the ex-cupbearer of the king.

Thanks to Joseph's efforts, the cupbearer was released. When the cupbearer returned to his job in the palace, instead of showing his gratitude to Joseph by putting in a good word for him with the King, the cupbearer totally forgot about his pal in prison. Joseph spent two more years locked up. I can only imagine what he was

217

feeling and thinking about his former cell mate and disloyal friend. If you were in his shoes, (or should I say chains?) how would you feel? Would you think that perhaps doing good was a waste of time and maybe you should never help anyone ever again?

Have you ever done favors for ungrateful people? It hurts when kindness is not appreciated or even acknowledged. Jesus knew that pain too. While walking through a town one day, he came upon ten men suffering from Leprosy. These men were outcasts. Nobody wanted to come near them for fear of catching the horrible disease. Lepers had to leave their families to live in quarantined colonies. Once diagnosed with leprosy, they could never touch another human being or be touched by anyone. Can you imagine how lonely they must have felt? And when they accidentally came close to someone, they were required to yell out "unclean!" so the person could get away from them. Talk about feeling rejected and unloved!

But there was someone who did care about these men. Jesus had compassion and healed them. Predictably, when the men were healed, they immediately ran to see their friends and families. In their excitement, nine of the ten forgot to even say thank you to Jesus. Only one returned to show his gratitude for receiving his life back.

If even Jesus was unappreciated for the good He did, we can't expect to receive any better treatment. People are thoughtless sometimes. It's easy to become angry and bitter when that happens, but neither Joseph the prophet nor Jesus the son of God reacted that way. They are examples for us to follow.

When we remember why we do good for others, it helps us forget about being forgotten. If we're doing good simply for the sake of doing good, our satisfaction won't depend upon the recipient's response.

We know that our acts of kindness are seen by God, so it doesn't really matter if anyone here on earth acknowledges what we've done. Our reward comes from the one we are seeking to imitate. His opinion is the one that counts.

And speaking of being forgotten and unappreciated, consider how much God has done for us that we don't remember to thank Him for!

May we keep our focus on the one
for whom we serve others, and may we never
forget to have an attitude of gratitude.

HAVE YOU WASHED YOUR SIEVE LATELY?

The Bible admonishes us to "fear not," but is freedom from fear really possible in this scary world?

We deal with some tough situations like caring for a critically ill child, losing a parent, struggling with financial or marital difficulties, or living with disabilities. Is it realistic to believe that we can transcend the cares and worries of this life? Dare we even hope to achieve peace of mind and total release from our burdens?

We know worry is a waste of energy. The Bible asks, "*Who of you by worrying can add a single hour to his life?*" (Matthew 6:27) It's futile to fret, and nobody really wants to worry; but with so many weighty concerns, how can we possibly obey the biblical command to not fear?

Perhaps we can eliminate fear by applying four P's.

The first "P" stands for planning. A wise person once said, "Hope for the best, but expect the worst." We don't want to be pessimists, but we should be aware that bad things are inevitable. Some Christians think God will keep anything bad from happening to them. This isn't true. The presence of trouble does not mean the absence of God. We all must plan to weather storms. God doesn't keep our boats out of the water; He just keeps the water out of our boats. If we have a plan of action decided upon before the need for it arises, fear won't take us by surprise.

The second "P" stands for pull. We need to pull fears out of our thoughts as if they were weeds and get them out before they take root and grow. We can replace them with the seeds of positive thoughts that will grow into flowers of peace. Rejecting fearful thoughts is tough, but Philippians 4:8 spells out a simple formula that enables us to replace fear with perfect peace: "*Whatever is true, whatever is honorable, whatever is right, whatever is pure, whatever is lovely, whatever is of good repute, if there is anything excellent and worthy of praise, let your mind dwell on these things."*

When we focus our attention on positive thoughts, fear is crowded out and has no room to grow. It's a simple concept, but that doesn't mean it's easy. It takes awareness to be mindful of the thoughts that pop into our heads. It takes diligence to consistently replace the negative thoughts with positive. This is where the third "P" comes in.

The third "P" stands for practice. We need to practice this new behavior until it develops into healthier, more positive thinking habits.

A friend once expressed the frustration she felt over her constant battle to put good thoughts into her mind. She lamented that although she was feeding her mind positive things by reading the Bible, she couldn't remember most of what she read. The discouraged lady felt as if her mind was a sieve into which God's word was flowing like water but then running out as quickly as it went in. I assured her that this was not cause for concern, because even when water flows out of a sieve, at least it's keeping the sieve clean. Though we may not remember Scriptures we read, by pouring them into our minds we keep our thoughts clean of negative worries and fears.

The fourth and final "P" stands for prayer. This one is critical, because we can do nothing in our own power. We need to constantly seek God's help.

"Do not be anxious about anything, but in everything, by prayer with thanksgiving, present your requests to God and the peace of God, which transcends all understanding, will guard your hearts and your minds in Christ Jesus." (Philippians 4:6-7 NIV)

A life free from fear is possible; but it requires a consistent effort to cleanse the sieve of your mind, washing it with the powerful, positive Word of God. Romans 12:2 says, *"Be transformed by the renewing of your mind."*

Fearless living requires dependence on God, the giver of true peace. *"Cast all your anxiety on Him because He cares for you."* (I Peter 5:7 NIV)

I am the Lord your God who takes hold of your right hand and says to you, do not fear. I will help you.
(Isaiah 41:13)

THERE IS NO "FUN" IN DYSFUNCTIONAL

What child doesn't like to imitate his parents? Little girls put on mommy's lipstick and little boys clomp around in daddy's shoes. Unfortunately, we often imitate bad habits of our parents too. Sometimes parents model negative behaviors that can ruin our lives if we imitate them. Addictions and abuse are behaviors that we would be better off not copying.

That's what dysfunctional families are all about—kids copying their parents—and hurting themselves and others as a result. And whose family is not dysfunctional?

We often find ourselves demonstrating behaviors we dislike. For some reason, it's much easier to pick up another's bad habits than it is to learn their good habits.

Once ingrained, negative traits and habits become like chains that are nearly impossible to break, but here's some good news: God says, *"You were redeemed from the empty way of life handed down to you from your forefathers."* (I Peter 1:18-19) In other words, there's hope of changing and ridding your life of some of those "empty ways" you learned while growing up. The dark stuff inside us—whether it's from our past or from our own choices—is wrapped up in what God calls "sin." Sin, simply put, is living in a way that's not good for us or those around us. It's falling short of the best God has planned for us.

Jesus died to not only forgive our sin—but also to break its power over us. He can remove those chains that bind us. He can change us from the inside out. No one has to stay stuck in dysfunctional lifestyles.

May we pray the prayer of King David in Psalm 51:10. *"Create in me a clean heart, oh God, and renew a right spirit within me."* Our "empty ways" have done enough damage. Continuing on in our mistakes will get us nothing but more pain. God is ready to transform our hearts, minds, and lives so we can enjoy the abundant life that Jesus came to give. With His transforming power in our lives, we can declare, "Dysfunctional behavior stops in this generation!"

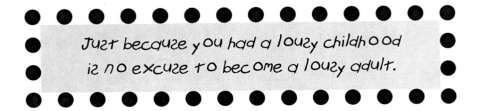

Just because you had a lousy childhood is no excuse to become a lousy adult.

IS BROCCOLI HAZARDOUS TO YOUR HEALTH?

Did you know that each time you eat broccoli, you're risking your life? According to a recent useless information poll, most of the people who die of cancer have eaten broccoli at some time in their lives. In addition, Dr. No Zetall of Dumstuff University in Oshkosh, Wisconsin reports that 99% of those in car crashes ate broccoli within six months of their accident. Prison surveys show that virtually all inmates were forced to eat broccoli as children. Scary, ha? With very few exceptions, all broccoli eaters born between 1800 and 1900 either are dead or have severe physical limitations. Holy cow! How come farmers don't stick warning labels on this dangerous stuff? You know I'm kidding; but have you guessed what I'm leading up to? You can add up the statistics and still make the wrong conclusion. The wrong focus can lead you way off track.

My grandson, Cobi focuses on the positive. He believes he can do anything. He's not afraid of failing or looking silly. He likes to show off his muscles and he brags about how tough he is. I once took him with me to the dentist. Having endured a traumatic experience when he was badly burned, he was terrified of all doctors' offices. The dentist tried to calm his fears by letting him operate the chair while I sat in it. He moved me up and down and tilted me to a reclining position. I asked if he'd like to try sitting in the chair.

"No way!" he said emphatically, shaking his head and taking a step backward. "But," he told the dentist, "when I grow up, I will be brave and not afraid to sit in that big chair under the hot light. I won't even care if my teeth are drilled," he said, "because I'm going to be big and strong, and tough and fearless . . . someday . . . when I grow up." Is it possible that I too can admit my present inadequacies and still have confidence that I will "grow up" some day? With God helping me, I will grow to be spiritually stronger, braver, and better in the future. This is what hope and faith are all about.

Kids only become pessimistic after we adults teach them that they can't do what they think they can. We begin life as positive thinkers. I believe God wants us to keep that positive, hopeful, trusting attitude.

A positive attitude is healthy. It keeps your spirits up. When things aren't going your way, you can remind yourself that someday things will get better.

Tomorrow you will get a better job, you'll meet Mr. Perfect, you'll lose that weight, and your bald spot will disappear. Well, maybe your bald spot won't disappear, and maybe there's no such thing as Mr. Perfect; but things will probably look better tomorrow anyway.

According to "they" (you know, the people who say everything), optimists are far less likely to develop heart disease than pessimists. I heard it was positive thinking that kept Dick Cheney's heart attacks down to only one per month.

"They" say optimists are more successful and happier than pessimists. The Bible confirms this idea. "*As a man thinks in his heart, so is he.*" (Proverbs 23:7) If you think of yourself as happy, loving, and capable, you will *be* happy, loving, and capable. If you believe you are a failure, you'll act like one and fulfill that prophecy about yourself. You become what you think you are.

Negative people may as well make reservations at the funeral parlor. Broccoli may not kill them, but focusing on the negative could. Pessimism causes ulcers and heart attacks, anxiety, and a host of other problems. Negativity, not vegetables, should carry a warning label.

A father who had heard
his son was in an accident said,
Pray that God will be good and let my son live.
His wife said, Isn't God good all the time?
God is what He is, no matter what's happening.

Dentist by Carissa S.

I'M WEAK!

"We are His workmanship created in Christ Jesus for good works, which God prepared beforehand that we should walk in them." (Ephesians 2:10)

Does this verse scare you? Do you worry about your ability to do the good works God wants you to do? If you're like me, you get frustrated and wonder whether you will ever "get it together." The answer is, "NOPE!"

We will never get it all together. But we don't have to, because God will. He has big plans for us. Even though we may consider ourselves to be useless vessels, He can do great things, as long as we have hearts that love Him and are willing to let Him work through us.

I'm reminded daily of how inadequate I am and how futile my attempts are to do and be "good." The apostle Paul had the same problem. He wrote in a letter to Roman Christians that he could not do what he wanted to do; and in spite of great effort to resist temptation, he continued to do the very thing that he hated doing. (Romans 7:15 & 19).

Remember the old Ajax commercial that said, "Its power is released in water?" Well, God's power is released in faulty human beings like me. 2 Corinthians 12: 9 says *"(His) Power is perfected in (my) weakness."*

Even in our weakness, God's strength will prevail. He will do through us what we are unable to do for ourselves. He will fill our inadequacies with His incomparable power. The greatness of our need allows Him to show the greatness of His power. We need to stop trying to do it in our own strength and let Him work.

If you're facing trials and feel weak and powerless, it's okay. You are in the perfect place for God to work through you and be glorified. *"I can do all things (that He gives me to do) through Him who strengthens me."* (Philippians 4:13)

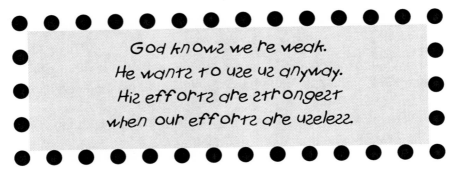

God knows we're weak.
He wants to use us anyway.
His efforts are strongest
when our efforts are useless.

UNDIE MAN TO THE RESCUE

Last night my grandson, Cobi, was putting his pajamas on in the bathroom when suddenly, the door swung open and he jumped out. Wearing his underwear on his head, he announced, "It's Undie Man to the rescue!"

Cobi loves super heroes. Last week when I bought him new shoes, his choice did not depend upon color, style, or comfort, but upon which super hero decorated the side of each shoe. When Cobi doesn't want to do something, like taking medicine, I suggest that a super hero could do it, and suddenly his attitude changes. He flexes his muscles, sticks out his chest, and transforms into a fearless boy who can do anything.

I could take a lesson from him. I'm no hero and I'm not super compared to anybody, but I can live fearlessly by reminding myself of the super heroes of faith. Their stories in both the Old Testament and the New Testament of the Bible illustrate how God's people have managed to live without fear in the past and how I can do it today.

The Bible admonishes us to "fear not" and to "be strong and courageous." These things are easy to talk about, but tougher to put into practice, especially when your life makes Job's look like a vacation in paradise.

David was hated and hunted by the King and his armies, yet he trusted God; and God took care of him. Paul was hated by leaders of the Jewish religion. He was captured, beaten, and imprisoned over and over, but he remembered that God was with him. That knowledge helped him get through it all. In a letter to the Corinthian church, Paul wrote, *"This all-surpassing power is from God and not from us."* (2 Corinthians 4:7)

When Jesus walked on the water toward the boat full of his apostles, Peter jumped out of the boat and headed toward him. (Matthew 14:28-30) He did well until he took his eyes off Jesus and looked around at the wind and the waves. Then he began to sink.

Peter knew Jesus had the power to help him walk on water, or he never would have left the boat; but he quickly forgot his goal when he saw how powerful the forces around him were. He needed a reminder to keep his eyes on Jesus. When he did that, he was fine and stayed above the waves.

We know God wants us to triumph in the midst of trouble. We know He's willing to give us the power to do it. We just forget sometimes because we're so busy looking at the problems that we take our eyes off the one who is stretching out His hand to help us.

When "Undie Man" emerges from my bathroom, I'm reminded to look to God for strength to live out the superhero life He's called me to. He provides power for me to leap over insurmountable obstacles that Satan puts in my way. I may not get a cape or an insignia on my chest, but God gives me everything I need to be victorious.

Sunshine by Brenna K.

When we maintain faith
and keep our focus on God's love
and the hope He has given us for eternity,
Christians can maneuver
the obstacle course of life.

THE SUNSHINE OF A WARM WORD

Two kids were talking one day. Marvin said, "That new kid in school is nothing but a big fathead!"

Matilda, in her refined way, softly said, "You shouldn't call people names like that. It's rude. I never call people names."

Marvin shrugged and told her, "Well, I just got mad when he said you were stupid looking." At this, Matilda put her hands on her hips and demanded, "What else did that big fathead say?"

It's easy to be kind to people who treat me well. The challenge is to practice kindness to those who are as friendly as a skunk backed into a corner. Sometimes I meet this challenge well and other times I fail miserably and feel lower than a pregnant pig's belly.

I still feel bad for being nasty to a neighbor of mine almost two years ago. Hopefully, she chalked it up to the fact that everybody has bad days (or for some of us, bad weeks, months, or years).

I hope that others will be patient with me, even on those days when I'm as lovable as a grizzly bear with a hangover. In the same way, I try to be considerate of others who might be having the worst day of their lives. When I encounter a crabby waitress, I try to smile more than usual and be extra nice to her. I comment on how hard she has to work and how she must tire of dealing with cranky customers. I give her genuine compliments on her service; and by the time I leave, she is usually smiling and wishing me a nice day.

With a kind word, you can drag an elephant by the tail. A little kindness goes a long way. I try to give people the benefit of the doubt. Chances are that the old grouch who snaps at you from behind the counter at Walgreens isn't the creepy monster of a man that you assume he is. Maybe he has problems you don't know about like fallen arches, false teeth that are too tight, itching psoriasis, or burning hemorrhoids. He might even have all of the above and more. If you had his problems, you'd probably be ornery and cantankerous too.

This world can be a cold place. Why not enhance global warming? What sunshine is to flowers, smiles and kind words are to humanity. The gift of a few kind words can warm three winter months. Don't you love it when someone warms your soul with a random act of kindness? Why not do the same for those you encounter? They might be in need of the warm sunshine of a kind word.

Super Hero by Rachel S.

Have a heart that never hardens,
a temper than never tires,
and a touch that never hurts.
(Charles Dickens)

WHAT THE WORLD NEEDS

My grandson was here for five days, and I lived to tell about it. The husband and I spent much of that time trying to impress upon Cobi that a diet of just pickles and olives is not balanced or healthy. Yesterday, he had three huge pickles for lunch . . . and that was all. He really loves salt.

Almost everybody likes salt. It's difficult to eliminate it from your diet when necessary. Without salt, everything tastes bland.

Life is pretty bland and tasteless too, without the "salt" of love. The Bible calls Christians the salt of the earth. Like salt, we should dive into the stew pot of the world and season it with the love of God.

I want to "walk in love," as the Bible says, but it's hard. I hate to admit it, but I act rude, bossy, judgmental, and harsh. I get impatient with people and I want my own way. Let's see, that would be called selfishness, wouldn't it? Ow.

In order to be more loving and therefore more like God, I need to remind myself of His awesome, undeserved, and unconditional love. This makes me more willing to reach out to others in the same way and share His love with them.

God's love flows freely to us, even though we don't deserve it. Does love also flow, like salt from a shaker, from us to others? The world really needs it.

By the way, when Cobi learned that pickles don't make muscles bigger, he decided that he wanted broccoli instead. As he ate it, I told him I could see his muscles growing. (Is it okay for grandmas to fib like that?)

Now I'm off to see what I can find for supper. I wonder if there are any pickles left.

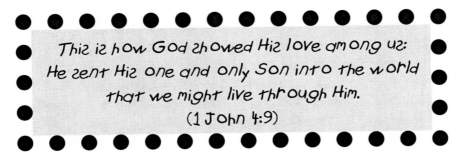

This is how God showed His love among us: He sent His one and only Son into the world that we might live through Him.
(1 John 4:9)

WHERE'S THE JOY?

You see the word "joy" around a lot, especially at holiday time. But many of us suffer with health problems, money problems, relationship problems, addictions, depression, or loss of a loved one. With such sadness, how can we know joy? Joy doesn't mean just feeling happy. Joy is that deep down peace in your heart you feel when you know things will be alright. We can have that kind of joy when we understand that:

* God promises never to leave or forsake us, if we seek Him.
* He can mend broken hearts and heal relationships.
* He can provide riches beyond what this world offers.
* He provided the perfect sacrifice for our sins.
* He offers us eternal life with Him, if we put our faith, trust, and hope in Him.

Don't let the cares of this world steal your joy. God sits on the throne hearing every prayer. He wants His children to have abundant life, and that means joy within. It doesn't come from outward situations. It comes from knowing your creator and believing His promises.

MY NEXT BOOK

I've already begun working on my second book, *Marriage for Dummies* or *The Clueless Husbands' Guide*.

Because the population of clueless husbands is increasing at an alarming rate, and because no one has adequately addressed this important issue, and (mostly) because I can't resist shoveling advice by the dump truck load, the time for this book has come!

I'm sure copies of this book will fly off the shelves at non-discriminating book stores as soon as they're available, so you may want to pre-order yours now.

This volume will include valuable advice on such topics as:

1) Why a husband should not park his Harley in the living room on the new Persian rug, even if it IS raining outside. (Yes, my husband really did this.)

2) What not to buy the wife for Christmas, such as tools, appliances, and windows. (Yep, I got a window for Christmas one year. Really!)

3) Why it is dangerous to hide chocolate from a menopausal wife who has run out of estrogen (unless you enjoy having your eyes poked out with a sharp stick).

4) Why it is imperative to your survival that you NEVER eat the last Ding Dong.

5) Why having your wife hold your drink while you play poker with your pals is not considered quality family time.

6) Why your wife never laughs at your jokes about her weight.

7) How to remove a rolling pin from your forehead after making jokes about your wife's weight.

8) How to have more in common with your wife than that you are both mammals who breathe oxygen.

9) Why nose picking is not sexy.

10) Why your wife is not impressed by flatulence.

11) What not to say to a wife with raging PMS after you have finished off the last of her triple fudge brownie delight ice cream with chocolate sprinkles.

12) Why wives don't appreciate a prize-winning burp when they hear one.

13) Why men are ten times more likely to visit emergency rooms with household objects embedded in their craniums.

The book will also include these special bonus sections: 1) Diagrams and step by step instructions on how to replace a toilet paper roll. 2) A pull-out centerfold map illustrating exactly where to put dirty underwear. 3) A list of some subtle telltale signs that your wife may have PMS:

a) Violent Yelling

b) Uncontrollable Sobbing

c) Severe Headache (after the cast iron frying pan whacks you in the back of the head)

d) The Hostess Bakery truck backs up to your front door to deliver Ding Dongs and Twinkies by the case.

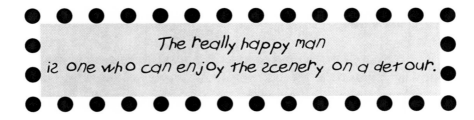

The really happy man is one who can enjoy the scenery on a detour.

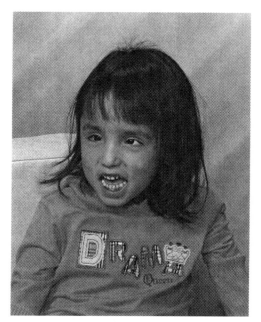

Tabitha Grace M.

Ronnie R.

Caleb L.

Tiara B.

Jimmy C.

Sarina S.

Elizabeth S.

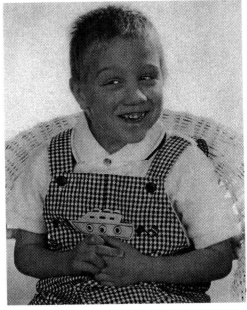

Michael H.

ABOUT THE AUTHOR

Marsha Jordan grew up in a suburb north of Chicago. Now a grandma, she lives in the north woods of Wisconsin with her husband of thirty years and their badly behaved toy poodle, King Louie, who rules the household with an iron paw.

She has suffered with migraines and battled depression for much of her life. Once an active volunteer and energetic mom, life as she'd always known it came to a screeching halt when she fell victim to a mysterious connective tissue disease that turned her life upside down. She knows how it feels to be sick, in pain, frustrated, and afraid.

In 2000, Jordan founded a non-profit charity for sick children. Through her Hugs and Hope Club, Jordan strives to send a message that God cares about our pain, and no one must face life's problems alone. She wants everyone everywhere to understand how much God desires to be intimately involved in our lives, help us through struggles, and have a personal relationship with each one of us. Jordan likes to remind people that God has a plan for every life and no one is insignificant. She encourages hurting people to learn of the awesome love, peace, and joy available to those who seek God and serve Him.

The author's stories have been published in several books, including *A Cup of Comfort*. Her essays have been featured in *Heart Light* and *Obadiah* magazines, as well as over thirty newsletters and online publications such as *Heart Warmers, Power to Share, Heart Touchers,* and *Warm Fuzzy Stories.*

Her web site has featured hundreds of kids with critical illnesses who have received thousands of cheery cards as a result. You can email her at hugsandhope@gmail.com or visit the web site at www.hugsandhope.org

Marsha Jordan

You see the word "joy" around a lot, especially at holiday time. But many of us suffer with health problems, money problems, relationship problems, addictions, depression, or loss of a loved one. With such sadness, how can we know joy? Joy doesn't mean just feeling happy. Joy is that deep down peace in your heart you feel when you know things will be alright. We can have that kind of joy when we understand that:

* God promises never to leave or forsake us, if we seek Him.
* He can mend broken hearts and heal relationships.
* He can provide riches beyond what this world offers.
* He provided the perfect sacrifice for our sins.
* He offers us eternal life with Him, if we put our faith, trust, and hope in Him.

Don't let the cares of this world steal your joy. God sits on the throne hearing every prayer. He wants his children to have abundant life, and that means joy within. It doesn't come from outward situations. It comes from knowing your creator and believing His promises.

I'm always looking for joy boosters and hope builders, so if you've found a joke, a poem, a stress buster, or a quote that has encouraged you or given you a smile, send it to me! It may end up on the HUGS and HOPE Club's web site.

The HUGS and HOPE Club for Sick Children, a 501(c)3 charity is committed to putting smiles on the faces of critically ill children. Since 2000, the group has been providing cheery cards, birthday and Christmas gifts, teddy bears and Bibles to children who are homebound or hospitalized. If you know of an injured or seriously ill child who might benefit from the HUGS and HOPE programs, contact us at or hugsandhope@gmail.com.

Everyone of any age or skill can be involved in spreading joy to kids with cancer and other life-threatening diseases. All it takes is a postage stamp. To learn about the children who could use cheery mail, visit the HUGS and HOPE web site at www.hugsand-hope.org.